# THE SKINNY SWEET air fryer COOKBOOK

## 75 GUILT-FREE RECIPES FOR DOUGHNUTS, CAKES, PIES, AND OTHER DELICIOUS DESSERTS

## ella sanders

CASTLE POINT BOOKS

NEW YORK

THE SKINNY SWEET AIR FRYER COOKBOOK.
Copyright © 2024 by St. Martin's Press.
All rights reserved. Printed in the United States of America.
For information, address St. Martin's Publishing Group,
120 Broadway, New York, NY 10271.

www.castlepointbooks.com

The Castle Point Books trademark is owned by Castle Point Publishing, LLC.
Castle Point books are published and distributed by St. Martin's Publishing Group.

ISBN 978-1-250-28216-3 (paper over board)
ISBN 978-1-250-32441-2  (ebook)

Design by Joanna Williams
Production by Mary Velgos
Photography under license from Shutterstock.com

Our books may be purchased in bulk for promotional, educational, or business use.
Please contact your local bookseller or the Macmillan Corporate and Premium Sales
Department at 1-800-221-7945, extension 5442, or by email at
MacmillanSpecialMarkets@macmillan.com.

First Edition: 2024

10 9 8 7 6 5 4 3 2 1

# contents

# skinny sweet satisfaction

If you think that healthy eating requires you to live in serious denial of all your sweet cravings, it's time to turn a new page . . . and the pages of this cookbook! In fact, if weight loss is your aim, some research suggests that including a few well-chosen treats in your weekly menu may actually help you reach your goals faster. That's because most restrictive diet plans can eventually grow boring, creating a downward spiral of stress and frustration that leads to a "cheating" mindset that causes you to abandon your goals.

But what if you had a range of delicious desserts to include in your menu? Occasional treats to look forward to when the desire for something sweet hits? This collection is packed with 75 perfect solutions for satisfying your sweet tooth without compromising your healthy goals. You'll enjoy Frosted Fruit Toaster Tarts (page 16), Small-Batch Chocolate Chip Cookies (page 90), Vanilla Dream Mini Cupcakes (page 114), and many more luscious yet light recipes.

## lighten up with your air fryer

Once you try just a few sweets and treats featured in the chapters that follow, you'll soon see how your air fryer can become an incredibly effective appliance to help you manage your weight. Here are the tried-and-true weight-loss strategies that have been incorporated into the recipes.

**Stick to right-size portions.** Who wouldn't be tempted to overindulge with a standard batch of three to four dozen cookies ready to be devoured? Your air fryer comes to the rescue with built-in portion control because of its relatively small size. Using an air fryer to make dessert means you can only prepare a few servings at a time. Weight-loss experts refer to this strategy as "the power of the pause" because you are literally building some decision time into your eating plan and avoiding a scenario where you have an overabundance of sweets on hand.

**Make smart substitutions.** Ingredients matter, and so you may be surprised to find recipes that use real butter and sugar in this collection. However, we're careful to use just enough to ensure great results. We've also incorporated ingredients that supply plenty of fiber (like oatmeal and fresh fruit and fruit butters) and protein (hello, Greek yogurt) when it makes sense to do so. Boosting fiber and protein intake and lowering the fat (and calories) in your dessert repertoire is key to making your sweet creations as healthy as possible.

# THE POWER OF MACROS

Beyond counting calories, balancing your macronutrients (macros)—fat, protein, and carbs—can help manage your weight. You can find recommended percentages of your daily diet for each macro through fitness and nutrition tracking apps that take into account your current weight, activity level, and goals.

**Fat:** One gram of fat contains 9 calories—more than twice the calories you get from the same amount of protein or carbs—so choose and use fats judiciously. Often, just a touch of fat will give you all the flavor and satisfaction you need, as you'll see in the recipes throughout this cookbook. Some fats, like the monounsaturated fats found in olive oil and nuts, are considered heart-healthy foods. Try to minimize saturated fats and steer clear of trans fats.

**Protein:** It's the building block your body needs to build muscle, and it plays an important role in helping to control your appetite and keep your metabolism humming. Some protein-rich foods are also high in fats, so scout out the leanest sources and keep smart portions in mind.

**Carbs:** They help your body perform many functions, but where weight loss is concerned it's helpful to think of carbs as a kind of fuel supply that comes in several different grades. Complex carbohydrates—including whole grains and fruits—are like high-grade fuel that your body burns more slowly. They also contain fiber, which is especially beneficial for weight loss because it helps you feel full longer.

# MORE TIME FOR YOU

Don't underestimate the power of your air fryer to put more time on your side! Air fryers tend to speed up cooking time for most recipes. The circulation of hot air means foods cook faster. And because most air fryer baskets come with a nonstick coating, cleanup is a breeze. You'll find more time to get out and enjoy an active lifestyle instead of waiting on your sweet creations and doing dishes. (Just be sure to always follow your manufacturer's safety instructions for proper care and cleaning of your air fryer.) Some great ways to spend the time you gain:

- Walk with a friend or canine buddy.
- Get out in the garden.
- Deliver some sweets on foot to your local fire station.
- Play pickleball.
- Explore your neighborhood or a local park by bike.
- Shoot some hoops or play tag with the kids or grandkids.
- Go birdwatching.
- Learn the latest social media dance trend.
- Hit some golf balls.
- Take to the water for swimming or kayaking.

**Keep it simple and flavor-packed.** Mother Nature has blessed us with her own version of candy, so you'll find plenty of fruit-based desserts to choose from in the pages of this cookbook. In general, any cooking process reduces a fruit's water content and thereby intensifies its natural sweetness. Enjoying a strong, concentrated flavor is more likely to leave you satisfied with fewer bites, so we've employed that logic in most of the recipes you'll find here.

## get the best results

Air fryers circulate hot air to cook, giving you faster, more even heat—and delicious results. When used in place of traditional deep frying, air fryers cut the fat and calories yet keep recipes tasting moist and rich on the inside and crispy on the outside. Although these appliances can vary greatly in their sizes and features, they can all give you amazing ease and taste. A few tips for getting the best from your air fryer:

**Know your tools.** If your air fryer has a cooking basket with removable racks, it's just a matter of pressing a few buttons to release the basket and load in your ingredients. Some air fryers even come with a baking pan for pizzas and desserts. If you don't have a baking pan designed for your air fryer, a glass, silicone, or oven-safe metal dish will work as long as it fits safely in the dimensions of your air fryer.

**Adjust as needed.** When it comes to timing and temperature, because the size of the basket can vary, for best results it's always a good idea to pay close attention to whatever you have in the air fryer and adjust your cooking time accordingly. Some recipes in this cookbook call for preheating when a blast of high heat improves the final results. However, other times it's easiest to load your dish into a cool air fryer basket.

Whether or not you'll need to always preheat your air fryer depends on which model you have, so check the instructions that came with yours. In general, preheating isn't necessary. But when it is, it only takes about 3 minutes.

**Keep it safe.** Despite the fact that an air fryer may be one of the most convenient, easy-to-use appliances in your kitchen, they are also powerful machines, so make sure you follow your manufacturer's safety recommendations carefully. Always use caution when adding ingredients to a hot basket or removing the basket after the cooking cycle, and make sure you place the basket only on heatproof surfaces.

Ready to dig in? Every recipe in this cookbook has been designed with your air fryer and weight loss in mind, so fitting skinny indulgences into your days is simple. Macro and calorie counts are included to help you stay on track with your treats. (Keep in mind that optional ingredients are not included in the nutritional analysis.) So start enjoying guilt-free desserts while making your way toward a new you—*The Skinny Sweet Air Fryer Cookbook* will share the secrets!

# breakfast treats

# Vanilla Glazed Doughnuts

**Makes 4 doughnuts** • **Prep time: 10 minutes** • **Total time: 20 minutes**

## DOUGHNUTS

1 cup all-purpose flour, plus more for dusting

1½ teaspoons baking powder

½ teaspoon salt

¾ cup vanilla nonfat Greek yogurt

## GLAZE

½ cup powdered sugar

1 tablespoon unsalted butter, melted

½ teaspoon pure vanilla extract

1½ teaspoons hot water

1 or 2 drops food coloring (optional)

Sprinkles (optional)

When only a doughnut will do, turn to your air fryer! The typical glazed doughnut, fried the old-fashioned way, can have more than 14 grams of fat and less than 5 grams of protein per serving. This air-fried version has only a quarter of the fat (and the calories that come with it) plus extra protein, thanks to the fat-free Greek yogurt.

**1.** Preheat the air fryer to 350°F.

**2.** To make the doughnuts: In a large bowl, stir together the flour, baking powder, and salt. Add the yogurt and mix until shaggy, then knead in the bowl until the dough holds together in a ball.

**3.** Divide the dough into four equal pieces. On a lightly floured work surface, roll each piece into a ball and pat into a disk about ½ inch thick. Poke your finger through the center of each disk to form into a doughnut shape.

**4.** Arrange the donuts in a single layer in the air fryer basket, with space between them. Spray the donuts lightly with cooking spray. Air fry for 7 minutes, pausing halfway through the cooking time to flip the doughnuts, until golden brown.

**5.** To make the glaze: In a small bowl, mix together the sugar, butter, vanilla, and water until smooth. Stir in the food coloring (if using). When the doughnuts are cool enough to handle, dip them into the glaze and top with sprinkles (if using).

*Per doughnut: 230 calories, 7 g protein, 42 g carbohydrates, 3 g fat (1.9 g sat fat), 1 g fiber*

# Chocolate Doughnuts

**Makes 6 doughnuts • Prep time: 20 minutes • Total time: 40 minutes + rising time**

½ cup whole milk, warmed

½ cup granulated sugar, divided

2¼ teaspoons active dry yeast

3 tablespoons salted butter, melted

1 large egg

1 teaspoon pure vanilla extract

1¾ cups all-purpose flour, plus more for dusting

¼ cup Dutch-processed cocoa powder

¼ cup powdered sugar

Freshly brewed coffee and homemade chocolate doughnuts are the perfect pair to start your morning on a slightly indulgent note. To sleep in longer, make the dough the night before, then cover and refrigerate. In the morning, just roll the doughnuts out to form. When they've risen again, a few minutes in the air fryer is all you need to make the magic happen.

**1.** In a large bowl, stir together the milk, 2 tablespoons of the granulated sugar, and the yeast. Let the mixture sit for 5 to 10 minutes, or until the yeast becomes foamy.

**2.** Add the butter, egg, vanilla, and remaining granulated sugar; stir until thoroughly combined.

**3.** Add the flour and cocoa powder. Using a silicone spatula or wooden spoon, mix until just combined, with no floury streaks.

**4.** Transfer the dough to a floured surface and knead it gently for 2 to 3 minutes, or until it forms a soft and slightly tacky dough.

**5.** Transfer the dough to a lightly oiled bowl and set it in a warm place to rise until almost doubled in size, about 1 hour. Alternatively, cover and refrigerate overnight.

**6.** On a lightly floured work surface, roll the dough out until it is ¼ to ½ inch thick, depending on desired doughnut thickness.

**7.** Use a 3-inch round cookie cutter to cut six doughnuts out of the dough. Poke your finger through the center of each disk to form into a doughnut shape. Arrange the doughnuts on a sheet pan and place them in a warm spot to rise for an additional hour.

**8.** Arrange the doughnuts in a single layer in the air fryer basket, with space between them. Air fry at 300°F for 7 to 8 minutes, flipping halfway through, until the doughnuts are soft on the inside and slightly crisp on the outside. Transfer the doughnuts to a wire rack to cool before sprinkling with powdered sugar.

*Per doughnut: 300 calories, 7 g protein, 53 g carbohydrates, 8 g fat (4.6 g sat fat), 3 g fiber*

# Apple Cider Doughnuts

**Makes 12 doughnuts** • **Prep time: 15 minutes** • **Total time: 40 minutes**

1 tablespoon + 1⅓ cup sugar, divided

1¼ teaspoons ground cinnamon, divided

1 cup white whole-wheat flour

½ teaspoon baking powder

¼ teaspoon salt

¼ teaspoon ground allspice

1 large egg

2 tablespoons unsalted butter, melted

½ cup apple cider

1 cup finely chopped peeled apple

Your air fryer, apple cider, and a touch of spice make breakfast nice! You'll need two silicone doughnut pans for this recipe because there's really no dough—it's a batter thanks to the cider that's added near the end. If you don't have a doughnut pan, these work well in regular muffin tins, too, although you may need to add a few minutes to the air frying time.

**1.** Preheat the air fryer to 350°F. Spritz two 6-cup silicone doughnut pans with vegetable oil.

**2.** In a small bowl, combine 1 tablespoon of the sugar and ½ teaspoon of the cinnamon. Set aside.

**3.** In a large bowl, whisk together the remaining ⅓ cup sugar and ¾ teaspoon cinnamon with the flour, baking powder, salt, and allspice.

**4.** In a medium bowl, whisk together the egg, butter, and cider.

**5.** Mix the wet ingredients into the dry ingredients until just combined, with no floury streaks. Fold in the apple.

**6.** Fill each prepared doughnut cup with a scant 2 tablespoons of batter.

**7.** Working in batches, place one pan of doughnuts in the air fryer basket. Air fry for 10 minutes, or until a wooden pick inserted into the center comes out clean. Let cool in the pan for 2 minutes, then tap out onto a wire rack. Repeat with the remaining pan.

**8.** Dredge the warm doughnuts in the reserved cinnamon-sugar mixture to coat.

*Per serving (2 doughnuts):* *175 calories, 4 g protein,*
*33 g carbohydrates, 3 g fat (1.5 g sat fat), 3 g fiber*

# Frosted Fruit Toaster Tarts

**Makes 4 tarts • Prep time: 15 minutes + rest time • Total time: 45 minutes**

1½ cups almond flour

¼ cup old-fashioned oats

1 tablespoon granulated sugar

¼ teaspoon baking soda

¼ teaspoon sea salt

2 tablespoons unsalted butter, cut into 3 or 4 pieces

1 egg white

2 tablespoons fruit jam

¼ cup powdered sugar

¼ teaspoon pure vanilla extract

1 or 2 drops food coloring (optional)

Sprinkles (optional)

Sweeten your day with a smarter version of that classic iced toaster pastry. Delicious and easy to make in your air fryer, these tarts have about half the carbs, quadruple the fiber, and three times as much protein compared with the store-bought variety. They're sure to satisfy morning, noon, or night!

**1.** Cut a piece of parchment paper into four 5-inch squares. Cut two more larger pieces for rolling the dough. Set aside.

**2.** In the work bowl of a food processor fitted with a metal blade, combine the almond flour, oats, granulated sugar, baking soda, salt, and butter. Pulse for 10 to 15 seconds, until the oats are finely chopped and the mixture has a fine, sandy consistency. Transfer the mixture to a large bowl. Add 1 tablespoon egg white and mix with clean hands until thoroughly combined. (It will be crumbly at first, but with a little extra mixing it should hold together in a ball.) Cover and refrigerate for 30 minutes.

**3.** Divide the dough into four balls. Working one at a time, place a ball of dough between the two larger pieces of parchment paper and roll into a thin rectangle (about 4½ x 7 inches). Remove the top piece of parchment and use a pizza cutter to cut the dough into two shorter pieces (about 3½ inches long).

**4.** Use a flat metal spatula to transfer one of the rectangular pieces to one of the 5-inch square sheets of parchment. Brush the edges with egg white and use the back of a spoon to spread about 1½ teaspoons of jam in the center, leaving a ½-inch margin of dough around the edges. Set the other piece of rolled dough on top, use the tines of a fork to gently press the edges together, and then poke a few holes into the top piece of the tart. Repeat with the remaining ingredients.

**5.** Working in batches if necessary, arrange the tarts in a single layer in the air fryer basket. Air fry for 12 minutes at 350°F until golden brown. Transfer the tarts to a wire rack and let cool.

**6.** To finish the tarts, in a small bowl, combine the powdered sugar, about a teaspoon of water, the vanilla, and the food coloring (if using). Stir until smooth, then spread evenly over the tarts. Top with sprinkles (if using).

*Per tart: 380 calories, 13 g protein, 36 g carbohydrates, 21 g fat (3.7 g sat fat), 4 g fiber*

# French Toast Rolls

Makes 4 rolls • Prep time: 10 minutes • Total time: 20 minutes

1 apple, peeled, cored, and cut into thin wedges

1 tablespoon sugar

1 large egg

2 tablespoons reduced-fat milk

Pinch of ground cinnamon

1 tablespoon peanut butter

1 tablespoon pure maple syrup

4 slices wheat bread, crusts removed

Enjoy the flavor of French toast any day of the week! The time-saving secret: Step away from the stove and let your air fryer do the work. Even if your kitchen tends to feel like Grand Central Station in the morning, you can ease into the day with this satisfying breakfast. Whether you sit and savor or take on the go, these French toast rolls will provide 10 grams of protein.

**1.** Sprinkle the apple slices with sugar and place on a piece of parchment paper in the air fryer basket. Air fry at 380°F for 5 minutes, until the apples are beginning to brown. Remove the apples from the air fryer and let sit until they are cool enough to handle.

**2.** Meanwhile, in a shallow bowl, whisk together the egg, milk, and cinnamon; set aside.

**3.** In a small bowl, stir together the peanut butter and syrup until smooth; set aside.

**4.** To assemble the rolls, use the palm of your hand to lightly flatten each piece of bread. Place a line of apples along the center of each piece, then roll one edge over the other to enclose the apples.

**5.** Dip each roll in the egg mixture, turning to coat, and then place seam-side down on another piece of parchment paper. Carefully place the parchment in the air fryer basket and air fry at 360°F for 5 to 7 minutes, until lightly browned.

**6.** Drizzle with the peanut butter–maple syrup mixture before serving. Or pack the drizzle to go in a dipping container.

*Per serving (2 rolls): 305 calories, 10 g protein, 49 g carbohydrates, 8 g fat (2 g sat fat), 4 g fiber*

# Caramelized Banana Oatmeal

**Makes 2 servings** • **Prep time: 5 minutes** • **Total time: 10 minutes**

1 large banana, sliced into ½-inch rounds

1 tablespoon unsalted butter, melted

1 tablespoon packed brown sugar

¼ teaspoon ground cinnamon

Pinch of salt

1 cup quick-cooking oats

1 tablespoon creamy peanut butter

2 tablespoons vanilla creamer (optional)

Oatmeal is a terrific breakfast food that provides a good helping of fiber and more protein than most grains. However, without a little oomph, it can be pretty bland. Your mornings deserve better! Fortunately, your air fryer can quickly transform a humble banana into a sweet topping that will make your oatmeal shine.

**1.** In a medium bowl, combine the banana, butter, brown sugar, cinnamon, and salt. Toss gently until the bananas are evenly coated.

**2.** Scatter the bananas in an even layer in the air fryer basket. Air fry at 400°F for 4 minutes.

**3.** Meanwhile, cook the oatmeal according to package instructions.

**4.** Stir the peanut butter into the oatmeal. Top with the banana slices and vanilla creamer (if using).

*Per serving: 340 calories, 8 g protein, 52 g carbohydrates, 13 g fat (5 g sat fat), 6 g fiber*

# Banana Soufflé

**Makes 2 servings** • **Prep time: 5 minutes** • **Total time: 20 minutes**

1 scant teaspoon
unsalted butter

1 teaspoon
granulated sugar

2 bananas,
coarsely chopped

2 large eggs

½ teaspoon ground
cinnamon

1 tablespoon powdered
sugar (optional)

Elevate your morning with a soufflé! Unlike traditional soufflé recipes, this batter comes together in just minutes and three steps. Your air fryer will whip up a glorious breakfast treat—crispy on the outside and fluffy on the inside—while you simply sip your coffee. For a bigger brunch offering, serve with fresh fruit and center-cut bacon.

**1.** Rub the inside of two 8- to 10-ounce ramekins with butter and sprinkle granulated sugar evenly on the bottom and sides, discarding the excess. Preheat the air fryer to 360°F.

**2.** In a blender, combine the bananas, eggs, and cinnamon. Pulse until smooth.

**3.** Pour the soufflé mixture into the prepared ramekins and carefully place the ramekins in the air fryer basket. Air fry for 15 minutes, until the soufflés are golden and firm. Serve immediately sprinkled with powdered sugar (if using).

*Per serving: 235 calories, 8 g protein, 30 g carbohydrates, 11 g fat (5.3 g sat fat), 3 g fiber*

# Blueberry Muffins

**Makes 6 muffins • Prep time: 10 minutes • Total time: 20 minutes**

1 large egg

⅓ cup sugar

⅓ cup milk

2 tablespoons vegetable oil

1 teaspoon pure vanilla extract

1 cup all-purpose flour

1 teaspoon baking powder

¼ teaspoon salt

½ cup fresh blueberries

Blueberries are sweet little treasures! They're rich in antioxidants that promote heart health, so it's a good idea to include more of them in your daily menu—starting with breakfast. Air fryer muffins are especially forgiving if you've forgotten about your blueberry stash in the fridge for a few days. The berries will soften in these melt-in-your-mouth treats.

**1.** Preheat the air fryer to 300°F. Lightly spritz six silicone muffin cups with oil and set aside.

**2.** In a large bowl, whisk together the egg and sugar until thoroughly combined.

**3.** Add the milk, oil, and vanilla. Whisk until thoroughly combined.

**4.** Add the flour, baking powder, and salt. Stir just until combined, with no floury streaks. Fold in the blueberries.

**5.** Divide the batter evenly among the prepared muffin cups. Arrange the muffin cups in the air fryer basket and air fry for 20 minutes, until golden and a wooden toothpick inserted into the center of a muffin comes out clean.

*Per muffin: 185 calories, 4 g protein, 29 g carbohydrates, 6 g fat (1 g sat fat), 1 g fiber*

# Banana Muffins

Makes 10 muffins  •  Prep time: 10 minutes  •  Total time: 25 minutes

2 very ripe bananas

⅓ cup olive oil

1 large egg

½ cup packed brown sugar

1 teaspoon pure vanilla extract

¾ cup self-rising flour

1 teaspoon ground cinnamon

Classic comfort food to the breakfast rescue! For the sweetest flavor and moistest muffins, use super-ripe bananas. In no time, you'll be enjoying perfectly browned goodness from your air fryer. If you don't have self-rising flour handy, just substitute all-purpose flour and add ¾ teaspoon of baking powder, ¼ teaspoon of salt, and ¼ teaspoon of baking soda.

**1.** Preheat the air fryer to 320°F and lightly spritz the inside of ten silicone muffin cups with oil or cooking spray.

**2.** In a large mixing bowl, mash the bananas until creamy. Add the oil, egg, brown sugar, and vanilla. Stir well until thoroughly combined.

**3.** Sprinkle the flour and cinnamon on top and fold until just combined, with no floury streaks.

**4.** Divide the mixture evenly among the prepared muffin cups.

**5.** Working in batches if necessary, carefully place the muffin cups in the air fryer basket. Air fry for 15 minutes, or until the muffins are golden and a wooden toothpick inserted into the center of a muffin comes out clean.

**6.** Transfer the muffins to a wire rack to cool completely.

*Per muffin: 165 calories, 2 g protein, 23 g carbohydrates, 8 g fat (1.2 g sat fat), 1 g fiber*

# Date-Walnut Bread

**Makes 1 loaf (12 servings)**  •  **Prep time: 15 minutes**  •  **Total time: 1 hour and 5 minutes**

2½ cups
chopped dates

4 tablespoons
unsalted butter

1 cup boiling water

½ cup packed
brown sugar

1 large egg

1½ cups
all-purpose flour

1 teaspoon
baking soda

1 teaspoon
baking powder

1 teaspoon salt

1 cup chopped
walnuts

Dates are an intensely sweet dried fruit, so you only need a small amount of brown sugar in this recipe. While this bread offers a delicious way to start your morning, you'll find it's equally enjoyable as an afternoon snack with a cup of hot tea. If you like, individually wrapped portions will keep well in your freezer.

**1.** Preheat the air fryer to 350°F. Grease and flour a 9 x 5-inch loaf pan.

**2.** In a medium bowl, combine the dates and butter. Pour the boiling water over the date mixture and let cool.

**3.** Stir the cooled date mixture to break up any clumps. Add the brown sugar and egg; mix until well blended.

**4.** In a large bowl, combine the flour, baking soda, baking powder, and salt. Stir the flour mixture into the date mixture until just combined, with no floury streaks. Stir in the walnuts. Pour the batter into the prepared pan and place in the air fryer basket.

**5.** Air fry for 50 minutes, until a wooden toothpick inserted into the center comes out clean. After 10 minutes, gently turn the bread out of the pan onto a rack to cool. Cool completely before slicing into twelve equal portions.

*Per serving: 280 calories, 5 g protein, 45 g carbohydrates, 11 g fat (3.2 g sat fat), 4 g fiber*

# Zucchini Bread

**Makes 1 loaf (12 servings)** • **Prep time: 20 minutes** • **Total time: 1 hour and 20 minutes**

1½ cups all-purpose flour

2 teaspoons
ground cinnamon

½ teaspoon kosher salt

½ teaspoon
baking powder

¼ teaspoon
baking soda

¼ teaspoon
ground allspice

2 large eggs

1½ cups
grated zucchini

1 cup sugar

½ cup canola oil

1½ teaspoons pure
vanilla extract

1 teaspoon orange zest
(optional)

½ cup toasted pecans,
roughly chopped

½ cup old-fashioned oats

Sneak in a veggie at breakfast! If your air fryer is large enough to handle a standard loaf pan, this easy breakfast bread offers a good way to use a bumper crop of zucchini in the summer—without having to rely on a standard oven and heating up your whole kitchen. Adding nuts and oats boosts the nutrition profile, giving you healthy fats and whole grains.

**1.** Preheat the air fryer to 350°F. Line a 9 x 5-inch loaf pan with a piece of parchment paper so that the edges hang over the long sides of the pan. Coat the pan with cooking spray and set aside.

**2.** In a bowl, whisk together the flour, cinnamon, salt, baking powder, baking soda, and allspice; set aside.

**3.** In a large bowl, whisk together the eggs until pale and foamy. Add the zucchini, sugar, oil, vanilla, and orange zest (if using); whisk to combine. Add the flour mixture and whisk until just combined, with no floury streaks. Stir in the pecans and oats. Pour the batter into the prepared pan and smooth the top.

**4.** Place the loaf pan in the air fryer and air fry for about 1 hour, until golden brown and a wooden toothpick inserted into the center comes out clean. After 10 minutes, gently lift the bread out of the pan onto a rack to cool. Cool completely before slicing into twelve equal portions.

*Per serving: 290 calories, 4 g protein, 33 g carbohydrates, 17 g fat (1.6 g sat fat), 2 g fiber*

# sweet snacks

# Praline Almonds

**Makes 24 servings (about 2 tablespoons each)** • **Prep time: 10 minutes** • **Total time: 20 minutes**

1 large egg white

2 tablespoons water

1 teaspoon pure
vanilla extract

1 pound almonds

¾ cup granulated sugar

¾ cup firmly packed
brown sugar

Pinch of salt

Packed with protein and monounsaturated fats, nuts make a very satisfying snack food. You'll love the way your air fryer can render them sweet and crunchy without much effort on your part. While these almonds are enjoyable on their own, you can also use them as a special garnish on salads or as part of a cheese plate.

**1.** Lightly spritz the air fryer basket with vegetable oil and set aside.

**2.** In a large bowl, whisk together the egg white, water, and vanilla until the mixture is frothy.

**3.** Add the almonds and stir until the nuts are thoroughly coated with the egg mixture.

**4.** Add the granulated sugar, brown sugar, and salt and stir again until the nuts are coated.

**5.** Working in batches, if necessary, spread the almonds in a single layer in the air fryer basket (it's OK if the nuts are touching).

**6.** Air fry at 300°F for 10 minutes, pausing halfway through the baking time to shake the basket, until the nuts are brown and fragrant. Tip the nuts onto a plate and let cool before serving.

*Per serving: 165 calories, 4 g protein, 17 g carbohydrates, 10 g fat (0.8 g sat fat), 2 g fiber*

# Sweet & Crunchy Chickpeas

**Makes 6 servings (about ¼ cup each)** • **Prep time: 5 minutes** • **Total time: 20 minutes**

1 (15-ounce) can chickpeas, drained and rinsed

1 tablespoon coconut oil, melted

2 tablespoons honey

½ teaspoon ground cinnamon

Pinch of salt

Bored of popcorn? You'll want to try these roasted chickpeas in your air fryer. Part of the legume family, chickpeas offer both protein and fiber, which makes them a super snack choice when you're craving something with a little crunch. A touch of honey and cinnamon give them just the right kiss of sweetness. When you want to go zesty, try swapping in a Cajun spice blend.

**1.** Preheat the air fryer to 380°F.

**2.** Place the chickpeas in a large bowl and pat dry with a paper towel.

**3.** Add the coconut oil, honey, cinnamon, and salt, stirring until the chickpeas are thoroughly coated.

**4.** Lightly spritz the air fryer basket with vegetable oil. Spread the chickpeas in a single layer in the basket. Air fry for 12 to 15 minutes, pausing halfway through the baking time to shake the basket, until the chickpeas are golden brown.

**5.** Tip the chickpeas onto a plate and let cool before serving.

*Per serving: 100 calories, 3 g protein, 15 g carbohydrates, 3 g fat (2.1 g sat fat), 3 g fiber*

# Cinnamon-Sugar Apple Chips

**Makes 2 servings** • **Prep time: 15 minutes** • **Total time: 40 minutes + cooling time**

1 Gala apple

1 tablespoon unsalted butter, melted

1 tablespoon brown sugar

¼ teaspoon ground cinnamon

Looking for chips low in calories but big on flavor? Apple chips crisp beautifully in your air fryer. Just four simple ingredients are all you need. (A little incentive to visit your local farmers' market or go apple picking!) If you have a mandoline slicer, the useful tool will make prepping easy. When your chips are close to the same size, they'll cook more evenly in the air fryer.

**1.** Core the apple and slice it into ⅛-inch-thick disks.

**2.** Lay the apple slices on a clean work surface and drizzle with the melted butter, then sprinkle with the brown sugar and cinnamon.

**3.** Lightly spritz the air fryer basket with vegetable oil. Working in batches if necessary, arrange the apple slices in the air fryer basket, making sure they don't overlap. Air fry at 360°F for about 25 minutes, pausing halfway through the cooking time to shake the basket, until browned.

**4.** Tip the chips onto a plate and let cool for at least 15 minutes before serving. (They will become crispier as they cool.)

**Per serving:** *120 calories, 3 g protein, 16 g carbohydrates, 6 g fat (3.6 g sat fat), 2 g fiber*

# Banana Chips with Chocolate Dip

**Makes 2 servings** • **Prep time: 5 minutes** • **Total time: 15 minutes**

1 large banana

1 teaspoon avocado oil

Pinch of kosher salt

¼ cup semisweet
chocolate chips

1 teaspoon
unsalted butter

There are so many options for fruit and veggie chips for snacking, but bananas are one of the best! For the crispiest results, use bananas that are barely ripe and still quite firm. Enjoy the chips with chocolate dip or solo (only 80 calories per serving for just the chips). They also make a crunchy topping for salads and taste great folded into a wrap.

**1.** Preheat the air fryer to 350°F.

**2.** Peel and slice the banana into ¼-inch-thick disks. Place in a bowl and drizzle with the avocado oil, tossing to coat.

**3.** Working in batches if necessary, carefully arrange the banana slices in a single layer in the air fryer basket and sprinkle with kosher salt.

**4.** Air fry for 8 to 10 minutes, pausing halfway through the baking time to shake the basket, until browned.

**5.** Meanwhile, place the chocolate chips and butter in a small microwave-safe bowl and microwave on high for 30 to 45 seconds, until the chocolate is melted. Stir until smooth.

**6.** Tip the chips onto a plate and let cool before serving with the chocolate for dipping.

*Per serving: 200 calories, 2 g protein, 29 g carbohydrates, 11 g fat (5.3 g sat fat), 3 g fiber*

# Spiced Kiwi Chips

**Makes 2 servings** • **Prep time: 10 minutes** • **Total time: 25 minutes**

4 kiwis

¼ teaspoon
ground cinnamon

⅛ teaspoon
ground nutmeg

Packaged versions of these sweet little tropical fruits are popping up in more places. But it's easy to save money and air fry your own with just fruit and two spices surely in your cabinet right now. Don't worry about peeling the thin skins. The flavor is bland compared to the intensity of the fruit, and your chips will hold their shape better if you leave them on. The chips will become crispier as they cool.

**1.** Slice the kiwi into ⅛-inch-thick disks. Arrange the slices in the air fryer basket and sprinkle with the cinnamon and nutmeg.

**2.** Air fry at 320°F for 15 to 20 minutes, pausing every 5 minutes to shake the basket, until they appear dry.

**3.** Tip the chips onto a plate and let cool for at least 15 minutes before serving.

*Per serving: 95 calories, 2 g protein, 22 g carbohydrates, 1 g fat (0 g sat fat), 5 g fiber*

# Strawberry Chips with Yogurt Dip

**Makes 2 servings** • **Prep time: 15 minutes** • **Total time: 1 hour and 45 minutes**

10 large strawberries, washed and hulled

½ cup plain nonfat Greek yogurt

1 tablespoon honey

Air-fried strawberry slices are super on their own or with a yogurt dip for snacking. They can also garnish a variety of desserts—from sherbet, ice cream, and pudding to cupcakes and cheesecakes. Making the slices doesn't require much hands-on time, but the total time can vary according to the thickness of your slices and the moisture in the berries, so plan to peek in on their progress. Starting the temp at a higher level and then turning it down will give the berries a jump start.

**1.** Cut a piece of parchment paper to fit the air fryer basket and set aside. Preheat the air fryer to 350°F.

**2.** Use a paper towel to pat the strawberries dry. Slice the strawberries into ⅛-inch-thick pieces. Arrange them in a single layer on the parchment paper.

**3.** Carefully place the strawberries in the air fryer basket and reduce the heat to 200°F. Air fry for 1½ to 2 hours, pausing every 15 minutes to flip the berries, until the tops are dry.

**4.** Tip the berries onto a plate and let cool before serving with the yogurt drizzled with honey for dipping.

*Per serving: 95 calories, 6 g protein, 18 g carbohydrates, 0.5 g fat (0.1 g sat fat), 2 g fiber*

# Maple Coconut Chips

**Makes 8 servings (about ¼ cup each)** • **Prep time: 5 minutes** • **Total time: 20 minutes**

1 tablespoon pure
maple syrup

1 teaspoon
coconut oil, melted

½ teaspoon pure
vanilla extract

Pinch of salt

2 cups large
unsweetened
coconut flakes

If you're a fan of coconut, these chips are sure to make you happy! And they only require a few minutes in the air fryer to achieve a rich golden brown. Enjoy them by the small handful as a snack, or use them to add an interesting twist as a topping for fruit salad or oatmeal. The possibilities are endless. The chips can be stored in an airtight container at room temperature for up to a week.

**1.** Preheat the air fryer to 320°F.

**2.** In a large bowl, combine the maple syrup, coconut oil, vanilla, and salt. Stir until thoroughly combined.

**3.** Add the coconut and toss until the flakes are evenly coated with the syrup mixture.

**4.** Spread the coconut in an even layer in the air fryer basket. Air fry for 12 to 15 minutes, pausing to shake the basket every 3 to 5 minutes, until crispy and golden.

**5.** Tip the chips onto a plate and let cool before serving.

*Per serving: 145 calories, 1 g protein, 6 g carbohydrates, 14 g fat (11.9 g sat fat), 3 g fiber*

# Nut & Fruit Bars

**Makes 16 servings** • **Prep time: 10 minutes** • **Total time: 25 minutes + refrigeration time**

2½ cups old-fashioned oats

½ cup peanut butter

½ cup honey

½ cup coarsely chopped almonds

½ cup flaxseed

1 cup dried fruit, such as cherries, blueberries, or cranberries

Why rely on expensive premade snack bars when it's so easy to make your own? These bars almost qualify as a no-bake treat except that a quick pass through your air fryer renders the oatmeal so much more flavorful after it has been lightly toasted. And with 6 grams of fiber per serving, these can work as a quick grab-and-go breakfast in a pinch.

**1.** Spritz a 9 x 9-inch pan with vegetable oil and set aside.

**2.** Spread the oats in the largest baking dish that will fit in your air fryer. Air fry at 350°F for 10 to 15 minutes, pausing every 5 minutes to stir the oats, until golden brown.

**3.** Meanwhile, in a large bowl, combine the peanut butter and honey, stirring until smooth. Add the almonds, flaxseed, dried fruit, and toasted oats. Fold the ingredients together until the mixture is thoroughly combined.

**4.** Press the mixture into the prepared pan. Cover and refrigerate for at least 1 hour or preferably overnight. Cut into sixteen bars.

*Per serving: 275 calories, 6 g protein, 30 g carbohydrates, 16 g fat (7.3 g sat fat), 6 g fiber*

# Banana Chocolate Wontons

**Makes 6 servings** • **Prep time: 30 minutes** • **Total time: 40 minutes**

1 ripe banana

2 ounces Neufchâtel cheese, softened

24 wonton wrappers

½ cup mini chocolate chips

½ teaspoon ground cinnamon

Powdered sugar (optional)

Crispy, creamy, and sweet come together in this snack package! Wonton wrappers are traditionally boiled or fried, but they work great in the air fryer, too. They are a marvelous way to present bite-size ingredients in a fun little package. The classic banana-chocolate pairing always hits the spot.

**1.** In a large bowl, mash the banana and cheese together until smooth.

**2.** Working one at a time, place a wonton wrapper on a flat surface. Place about a dozen chocolate chips in the center of the wrapper and top with a small spoonful of the banana mixture.

**3.** Dip your finger into a bowl of water and moisten the edges of the wrapper. Fold in half along the diagonal to form a triangle and press the sides together to close completely. Bring the corners of the long edge together, dab with more water if necessary, and press to seal. Repeat with the remaining ingredients and then generously spritz the wontons with vegetable oil.

**4.** Working in batches if necessary, arrange the wontons in a single layer in the air fryer basket. Air fry at 330°F for about 4 minutes, until light brown.

**5.** Sprinkle with the cinnamon and powdered sugar (if using) before serving.

*Per serving (4 wontons): 205 calories, 5 g protein, 33 g carbohydrates, 7 g fat (4 g sat fat), 2 g fiber*

# Caribbean Wontons with Mango Dipping Sauce

**Makes 8 servings** • **Prep time: 30 minutes** • **Total time: 40 minutes**

1 ripe banana

2 ounces Neufchâtel cheese, softened

¼ cup dried pineapple, finely chopped

¼ cup sweetened shredded coconut

2 tablespoons chopped walnuts

24 wonton wrappers

**DIPPING SAUCE**

1 mango, peeled, seeded, and chopped

2 tablespoons honey

1 to 2 tablespoons lime juice (optional)

Want to get a little festive with fruit? These wontons are ready for a party! You can assemble them a few hours ahead of the event and then air fry them just before you plan to serve. Simply cover and refrigerate for a stress-free snack that is likely to have everyone asking for the recipe.

**1.** In a large bowl, mash the banana and cheese together until smooth. Add the pineapple, coconut, and walnuts, stirring until thoroughly combined.

**2.** Working one at a time, place a wonton wrapper on a flat surface. Place 2 small teaspoons of the filling in the center of the wrapper.

**3.** Dip your finger into a bowl of water and moisten the edges of the wrapper. Fold in half along the diagonal to form a triangle and press the sides together to close completely. Bring the corners of the long edge together, dab with more water if necessary, and press to seal. Repeat with the remaining ingredients and then generously spritz the wontons with vegetable oil.

**4.** Working in batches if necessary, arrange the wontons in a single layer in the air fryer basket. Air fry at 330°F for about 4 minutes, until light brown.

**5.** To make the dipping sauce: Place the mango, honey, and lime juice (if using) in the work bowl of a food processor. Whirl until smooth. Serve in a small bowl alongside the wontons.

*Per serving (3 wontons): 180 calories, 4 g protein, 32 g carbohydrates, 5 g fat (2.1 g sat fat), 2 g fiber*

# Chinese Sesame Balls

**Makes 6 servings** • **Prep time: 30 minutes** • **Total time: 1 hour**

½ cup sweet red bean paste

¾ cup + 1 tablespoon sweet white rice flour, divided, plus more for dusting

¼ cup sugar

Pinch of salt

4 tablespoons boiling water, divided

1 teaspoon canola oil

¾ cup white sesame seeds, not toasted

You may have relished these treats as part of a dim sum experience—their soft chewy texture and crisp nutty coating make them hard to forget. But you can enjoy them anytime! They are actually remarkably easy to make at home in your air fryer. You can find red bean paste online or in Asian markets.

**1.** Divide the bean paste into twelve portions and roll into balls (dust your hands with a bit of flour to make this easier). Set aside.

**2.** In a large bowl, whisk together ¾ cup of the flour, sugar, and salt until thoroughly combined. Add 2 tablespoons of the boiling water and use a silicone spatula to mix until the dough is cool enough to handle (it will be shaggy at this point).

**3.** Add the oil and knead the dough in the bowl until it is smooth and not sticky.

**4.** Place the dough on a lightly floured surface and shape it into a log. Divide into twelve equal portions and cover with a cloth to keep them from drying out as you work.

**5.** Working one at a time, flatten a portion of dough into a disk. Place a ball of bean paste in the center of the disk. Gather the edges to enclose, pinch to seal, and then roll the dough ball between your hands to make sure it is smooth and round with no cracks in the surface. (If cracks appear, dab with water and roll smooth.) Place the ball under the cloth and repeat with the remaining ingredients.

**6.** Preheat the air fryer to 320°F.

**7.** In a small bowl, combine the remaining 2 tablespoons of boiling water and the remaining 1 tablespoon of flour and whisk until smooth. Place the sesame seeds on a plate.

**8.** Working one at a time, dip the dough balls in the flour mixture and then roll in the sesame seeds until thoroughly coated. Spritz the sesame balls with vegetable oil and arrange in the air fryer basket so they are not touching.

**9.** Air fry for 15 minutes, pausing to shake the basket a few times, then increase the temperature to 350°F and continue air frying for 15 minutes longer, until the balls are golden brown. Let cool briefly. Serve warm.

*Per serving (2 balls): 260 calories, 7 g protein, 35 g carbohydrates, 12 g fat (1.7 g sat fat), 4 g fiber*

# Raspberry Toast

**Makes 2 servings** • **Prep time: 5 minutes** • **Total time: 10 minutes**

2 thin slices
whole-grain bread

1 tablespoon walnuts

1 tablespoon
sliced almonds

1 tablespoon
peanut butter

¼ cup fresh raspberries,
lightly mashed

1 tablespoon
sunflower seeds

Sometimes the simple things in life can be pretty sweet. Avocado toast is great, but when you're craving something sweet, turn to this toast. If you're considering getting rid of some appliances, you might want to ditch your toaster after putting together this quick and easy treat. Air fryers circulate heat evenly, whereas toasters rely on radiant heat, which can create hot spots on your food.

**1.** Arrange the bread in a single layer in the air fryer basket. Air fry at 400°F for 4 to 6 minutes, pausing halfway through the baking time to flip the bread, until golden. If you enjoy your nuts toasted, add them to the basket when you flip the bread.

**2.** Spread the peanut butter on one side of each slice and top with the raspberries, nuts, and seeds.

*Per serving: 240 calories, 8 g protein, 24 g carbohydrates, 14 g fat (1.8 g sat fat), 5 g fiber*

# rich & creamy dreams

# Cinnamon-Raisin Bread Pudding

**Makes 2 servings** • **Prep time: 15 minutes** • **Total time: 35 minutes**

2 large eggs

1 cup 2% reduced-fat milk

3 tablespoons sugar, divided

Pinch of salt

¼ teaspoon ground cinnamon

2 slices whole-wheat bread, preferably slightly stale, torn into 1½-inch pieces

3 tablespoons raisins

1 tablespoon honey

Reduced-calorie vanilla ice cream (optional)

Stale bread has a silver lining: this delicious pudding that can walk the line toward either breakfast or dessert! It's quick to assemble for a whole-wheat air fryer treat. For breakfast just skip the ice cream topping . . . or don't. No raisins on hand? Try substituting another dried fruit or some chopped apple instead.

**1.** Lightly spritz a small oven-safe baking dish (about 3-cup capacity) with oil and set aside.

**2.** In a large bowl, whisk together the eggs, milk, 2 tablespoons of the sugar, salt, and cinnamon until thoroughly combined.

**3.** Add the bread and raisins, stirring gently so the bread is thoroughly soaked in the egg mixture.

**4.** Transfer the mixture to the prepared baking dish. Sprinkle the remaining 1 tablespoon of sugar on top.

**5.** Place the baking dish in the air fryer basket and air fry at 350°F for 15 minutes, until the pudding is puffed and golden and the center is set. Carefully remove the pudding from the air fryer and let cool on a wire rack for 5 to 10 minutes.

**6.** Serve drizzled with honey and a small scoop of ice cream (if using).

*Per serving: 350 calories, 14 g protein, 57 g carbohydrates, 8 g fat (3.3 g sat fat), 2 g fiber*

# Dairy-Free Rice Pudding

**Makes 4 servings** • **Prep time: 5 minutes** • **Total time: 1 hour and 35 minutes + refrigeration time (optional)**

½ cup short-grain rice, preferably Arborio

½ cup sugar

4 cups almond milk

1 teaspoon pure vanilla extract

1 cinnamon stick

So many air fryer recipes rely on the appliance's ability to blast heat intense enough to mimic actual deep frying, but this recipe showcases the air fryer's softer side. A low, gentle heat is all you need to bring out the natural sweetness of rice and almonds in this stunningly simple dessert. Serve warm or chilled with fresh fruit.

**1.** Preheat the air fryer to 300°F.

**2.** Lightly butter a deep 6-cup ovenproof casserole dish that can fit in the air fryer basket.

**3.** Add the rice, sugar, milk, vanilla, and cinnamon to the dish. Mix slightly.

**4.** Carefully place the dish in the air fryer basket and air fry for 1½ hours, until the pudding has thickened and become golden.

**5.** Transfer the pudding to a wire rack to cool to room temperature. Remove the cinnamon stick. Cover and refrigerate before serving if chilled pudding is your preference.

*Per serving: 280 calories, 3 g protein, 61 g carbohydrates, 3 g fat (0 g sat fat), 2 g fiber*

# Chocolate Soufflé

**Makes 2 servings • Prep time: 20 minutes • Total time: 35 minutes**

½ teaspoon
unsalted butter

4 tablespoons granulated
sugar, divided, plus
1 teaspoon for the
ramekins

2 ounces plain dark
chocolate (at least
70% cocoa), chopped

2 large eggs, separated

½ teaspoon pure
vanilla extract

Powdered sugar,
for dusting

Fresh raspberries
(optional)

Got dark chocolate? Add just a few ingredients you're likely to have on hand and this impressive dessert can be yours to savor. It's a bit on the more indulgent side, but keeping the servings to just two small ramekins offers portion control. Single servings also make this dessert easy to create in your air fryer—instead of heating up your kitchen with the oven.

**1.** Preheat the air fryer to 330°F. Coat the insides of two 6-ounce ramekins with butter. Sprinkle ½ teaspoon of granulated sugar into each of the ramekins, shaking to spread around, then dump out the excess.

**2.** Set a large heatproof bowl over a pan of simmering water and add the chocolate (don't let the bowl touch the water). Stir continuously until the chocolate has melted. Remove from the heat.

**3.** In another bowl, combine the egg yolks with 2 tablespoons of the granulated sugar and the vanilla. Whisk until the mixture becomes creamy. Stir the egg mixture into the melted chocolate until thoroughly combined.

**4.** In the bowl of a stand mixer fitted with a whisk attachment, whip the egg whites at medium speed until they just hold soft peaks. Slowly add the remaining 2 tablespoons of granulated sugar while continuing to beat at medium speed, then increasing to high speed until the whites hold stiff peaks.

**5.** Using a silicone spatula, fold about half of the whites into the chocolate mixture to lighten it. Then add the chocolate mixture to the remaining whites, folding gently until no egg white streaks remain.

**6.** Divide the mixture between the prepared ramekins and arrange them in the air fryer basket. Air fry for 13 minutes, until the soufflés have risen and the tops barely jiggle as you move the basket.

**7.** Serve the soufflés in their ramekins, dusted with powdered sugar and topped with fresh raspberries (if using).

*Per serving: 345 calories, 9 g protein, 38 g carbohydrates, 18 g fat (8.9 g sat fat), 3 g fiber*

# Easy Tiramisu

Makes 4 servings • Prep time: 15 minutes • Total time: 30 minutes + refrigeration time

## LADYFINGERS

1 large egg, separated

1 tablespoon granulated sugar

¼ cup all-purpose flour

## CREAM

⅔ cup heavy whipping cream

2 tablespoons powdered sugar

4 ounces mascarpone (about ½ cup)

1 teaspoon pure vanilla extract

1 cup strong coffee or espresso

1 tablespoon granulated sugar

1 teaspoon Dutch-processed cocoa powder, divided

Here's a special occasion treat that is sure to please, and an excellent example of how your air fryer can save you time and money. Making your own ladyfingers in the air fryer only requires a few minutes and three basic ingredients. You can assemble this dessert in a small casserole dish if you want to serve it in square portions, or serve it in individual glasses as pictured.

**1.** To make the ladyfingers: In a stand mixer fitted with a whisk attachment, whisk the egg white and granulated sugar until stiff peaks form. Fold the yolk into the egg white until thoroughly incorporated. Sprinkle with the flour and fold again just until combined.

**2.** Transfer the dough to a resealable plastic bag and snip off one corner. On a parchment-lined baking sheet, pipe the dough into 2-inch-long tubes that will fit into the air fryer. Air fry at 330°F for 12 minutes, until golden brown. Transfer to a wire rack to cool.

**3.** To make the cream: In the bowl of a stand mixer fitted with a whisk attachment, whip the cream and powdered sugar for 1 to 2 minutes on high speed until stiff peaks form. Transfer the whipped cream to another bowl and set aside.

**4.** In the same mixing bowl, use a paddle attachment to whip the mascarpone and vanilla until creamy. Use a silicone spatula to gently fold the whipped cream into the mascarpone mixture until thoroughly combined.

**5.** To assemble: Combine the hot espresso and granulated sugar in a shallow dish and stir until the sugar dissolves.

**6.** Dip each ladyfinger in the espresso mixture, working quickly, and arrange half of them in a single layer in a 5 x 7-inch serving dish or in individual serving glasses.

Spread half of the cream evenly on top. Put ½ teaspoon of the cocoa powder in a small strainer and dust over the cream. Repeat with the remaining ladyfingers, cream, and ½ teaspoon cocoa powder.

**7.** Cover with plastic wrap and refrigerate for at least 6 hours, or preferably overnight, before serving.

**Per serving:** *275 calories, 4 g protein, 21 g carbohydrates, 20 g fat (12 g sat fat), 0 g fiber*

# Lemon-Ginger Cheesecakes

**Makes 6 servings** • **Prep time: 15 minutes** • **Total time: 40 minutes + refrigeration time**

6 gingersnaps, crushed

1 tablespoon unsalted butter, softened

1 (8-ounce) package Neufchâtel cheese, softened

¼ cup sugar

1 tablespoon all-purpose flour

1 lemon, zest and juice from half, remaining half thinly sliced into 6 rounds (optional)

1 tablespoon freshly grated ginger

1 large egg

6 tablespoons prepared lemon curd

Liven up your cheesecake with this flavor combination! The spicy gingersnap crust creates the perfect base for the lemon-ginger filling. Although it tastes rich and creamy, you can stay on track with your health goals by making individual portions in your air fryer. And the bright mini cheesecakes look gorgeous to serve to guests.

**1.** Preheat the air fryer to 350°F.

**2.** In a bowl, use a fork to mix the gingersnap crumbs and butter until thoroughly combined. Divide the crumb mixture evenly among six silicone muffin cups. Use the back of a spoon to press the crumbs firmly into the bottom and slightly up the sides of each cup.

**3.** In a large bowl, beat the Neufchâtel until creamy. Add the sugar, flour, lemon zest, lemon juice, and ginger; mix well. Add the egg; beat just until blended.

**4.** Divide the batter among the muffin cups, using the back of a spoon to smooth the tops. Carefully arrange the cheesecakes in the air fryer basket and air fry for 25 to 30 minutes, or until the centers are almost set. Transfer the cheesecakes to a wire rack to cool.

**5.** Cover and refrigerate the cheesecakes for at least 1 hour. To serve, remove the cheesecakes from the muffin cups and top each cheesecake with 1 tablespoon lemon curd and a lemon slice (if using).

*Per serving: 250 calories, 5 g protein, 25 g carbohydrates, 14 g fat (7.1 g sat fat), 0 g fiber*

# Chocolate Cheesecakes

**Makes 12 servings** • **Prep time: 15 minutes** • **Total time: 40 minutes + refrigeration time**

⅔ cup almond flour

4 tablespoons unsalted butter, melted

5 tablespoons powdered sugar, divided

2 tablespoons Dutch-processed cocoa powder, divided

1 (8-ounce) package Neufchâtel cheese, softened

1 large egg

½ teaspoon pure vanilla extract

¼ teaspoon salt

½ ounce unsweetened baking chocolate, melted

2 tablespoons heavy cream

Calling all chocolate lovers! These air fryer mini cheesecakes cook in less time than the traditional oven method and give you built-in portion control. Use the time you gain to get out for a walk before mindfully enjoying one of your new favorite desserts.

**1.** In a bowl, combine the almond flour, butter, 1 tablespoon of the powdered sugar, and 1 tablespoon of the cocoa powder. Whisk until thoroughly combined. Divide the mixture among twelve silicone muffin cups and use the back of a spoon to press the mixture firmly into the bottom and slightly up the sides of each cup.

**2.** Working in batches if necessary, place the muffin cups in the air fryer and air fry at 350°F for 7 minutes; remove from the air fryer and let the crusts cool completely on a wire rack.

**3.** In the bowl of a stand mixer fitted with a paddle attachment, beat the Neufchâtel, egg, remaining 4 tablespoons of powdered sugar, remaining 1 tablespoon of cocoa powder, vanilla, and salt until smooth.

**4.** Add the chocolate and heavy cream. Mix until combined.

**5.** Spoon the filling onto the cooled crusts.

**6.** Carefully arrange the cheesecakes in the air fryer basket and air fry for 15 to 18 minutes, or until the centers are almost set. Transfer the cheesecakes to a wire rack and let cool. Cover and refrigerate the cheesecakes for at least 1 hour before serving.

*Per serving: 150 calories, 5 g protein, 7 g carbohydrates, 12 g fat (6 g sat fat), 1 g fiber*

# Chocolate-Avocado Cream Horns

**Makes 6 servings** • **Prep time: 20 minutes** • **Total time: 30 minutes**

1 sheet frozen puff pastry, thawed overnight in the refrigerator

2 ripe avocados, peeled and pitted

¼ cup Dutch-processed cocoa powder

¼ cup pure maple syrup

1 teaspoon pure vanilla extract

Pinch of salt

Powdered sugar (optional)

Wrapped in puff pastry and filled with creamy chocolate goodness, these horns are heavenly! If you don't own cream horn molds, you can use mini ice-cream cones as the form instead; wrap them in a layer of foil. It's a little trickier, but two wooden skewers (trimmed as needed) can help shape a foil form as well. The fat and calories may look like a splurge, but a lot comes from healthy fat in the avocados.

**1.** Preheat the air fryer to 370°F.

**2.** On a lightly floured surface, roll out the puff pastry until it is flat (but not thin). Using a ruler and a sharp knife or a pastry wheel, cut the puff pastry into six equal strips.

**3.** Working one at a time, wrap each strip around a cream horn mold, overlapping the pastry a little as you go.

**4.** Working in batches if necessary, arrange the cones on parchment paper in the air fryer basket so that they don't touch (the pastry will expand as it bakes).

**5.** Air fry for 6 minutes, or until lightly golden. Let cool on a metal rack before removing the metal cones.

**6.** In the work bowl of a food processor, combine the avocado, cocoa powder, syrup, vanilla, and salt. Whirl for 1 to 2 minutes, until smooth. Transfer the avocado mixture to a resealable plastic bag and snip a small hole in the corner. Pipe the avocado filling into the horns. Dust with powdered sugar (if using) before serving.

*Per serving: 280 calories, 5 g protein, 35 g carbohydrates, 18 g fat (6.3 g sat fat), 5 g fiber*

# Cream-Filled Phyllo Cups

Makes 12 cups · Prep time: 10 minutes · Total time: 20 minutes

12 frozen phyllo cups

1 tablespoon unsalted butter, melted

2 tablespoons shredded sweetened coconut

⅓ cup heavy whipping cream

¼ cup powdered sugar

¼ cup mascarpone cheese

1 tablespoon pure vanilla extract

12 white chocolate–covered espresso beans

If you haven't already fallen in love with air-fried phyllo cups, this versatile recipe will convince you. Once you experience how simple it is to prepare the cups and fill them with creamy goodness, you open the door to so many inventive toppings. This version will get you started with a light sprinkle of toasted coconut and a white chocolate–covered espresso bean.

**1.** Brush the phyllo cups with melted butter and arrange in a single layer in the air fryer basket. Air fry at 300°F for 3 to 5 minutes, until golden brown. Transfer the cups to a serving platter and let cool to room temperature.

**2.** Place the coconut on a small piece of parchment paper and carefully place in the air fryer basket. Air fry at 300°F for 3 to 5 minutes, until golden brown. Set aside.

**3.** In the bowl of a stand mixer fitted with a whisk attachment, whip the cream and powdered sugar on high speed for 1 to 2 minutes, until stiff peaks form. Transfer the whipped cream to another bowl and set aside.

**4.** In the same mixing bowl, use a paddle attachment to whip the mascarpone and vanilla until creamy. Use a silicone spatula to gently fold the whipped cream into the mascarpone mixture until thoroughly combined.

**5.** Spoon the cream filling into the phyllo cups and top with the toasted coconut and espresso beans.

*Per serving (3 cups): 240 calories, 3 g protein, 19 g carbohydrates, 17 g fat (10.6 g sat fat), 0 g fiber*

# Sicilian Cannoli

**Makes 6 servings** • **Prep time: 25 minutes** • **Total time: 30 minutes + refrigeration time**

1 cup part-skim
ricotta cheese

1 cup all-purpose flour,
plus more for dusting

2 tablespoons
salted butter

1 large egg yolk

¼ cup marsala wine

½ cup powdered sugar,
plus more for dusting
(optional)

1 teaspoon pure
vanilla extract

This cream-filled Sicilian dessert favorite is typically made by deep-frying the shells. But why go that route when you can get reliably delicious and lower-fat results with your air fryer? You'll also have less mess to clean up. If you haven't yet invested in stainless steel cannoli tubes, you can easily find them online. Serve the cannoli with fresh berries.

**1.** Line a fine-mesh strainer with cheesecloth. Place the strainer over a bowl and add the ricotta to the strainer. Let the ricotta drain in the fridge for at least an hour or up to overnight while preparing the cannoli shells.

**2.** Add the flour and butter to the bowl of a food processor and pulse until the butter is the size of small peas. Add the egg yolk and marsala wine and pulse until the dough comes together in a large ball. Wrap the dough in plastic wrap and refrigerate for at least 30 minutes or up to overnight.

**3.** Preheat the air fryer to 400°F.

**4.** Roll the dough out on a lightly floured surface until it's ⅛ to ¼ inch thick. Cut six 3-inch circles from the dough; reroll and recut any scraps of dough as needed. Roll each piece of dough around a cannoli tube.

**5.** Working in batches if necessary, carefully arrange the shells in the air fryer basket so they are not touching. Air fry for 5 to 7 minutes, or until the shells are crisp. Carefully transfer to a wire rack and let cool completely before proceeding with the next step.

**6.** In a large mixing bowl, combine the strained ricotta, powdered sugar, and vanilla. Beat until the mixture is light and fluffy. Transfer the mixture to a piping bag fitted with a large round tip. Pipe the filling into the cannoli shells. Dust with additional powdered sugar (if using).

*Per serving: 245 calories, 7 g protein, 30 g carbohydrates, 8 g fat (4.8 g sat fat), 1 g fiber*

# Beetroot Brownies

**Makes 6 servings** • **Prep time: 20 minutes** • **Total time: 2 hours**

1 large beet

¼ cup semi-sweet chocolate chips, melted, + 2 tablespoons unmelted

2 tablespoons pure maple syrup

1 large egg

½ teaspoon pure vanilla extract

½ cup almond flour

3 tablespoons Dutch-processed cocoa powder

¼ teaspoon baking soda

¼ teaspoon baking powder

Pinch of salt

If you love chocolaty brownies, this dessert is a game changer! Many recipes rely on all kinds of fruit purees to boost nutritional benefits and lower the amount of unnecessary fats. But have you ever considered baking some vegetables into your dessert instead? Beets are one of the best to try—especially when your air fryer can do double duty by first giving you an easy way to roast your beet and then baking the ultimate, rich results!

**1.** Wrap the beet in foil and place in the air fryer basket. Air fry at 400°F for about an hour, until softened. Unwrap the foil and let cool until the beet is easy to handle, then slip off the skin and chop into a few large pieces. Place the beet in the bowl of a food processor and whirl for about a minute, until the beet is a smooth paste consistency. Measure ¼ cup of beet puree and save the rest for another use.

**2.** Line a 9 x 5-inch loaf pan with a piece of parchment so that the paper hangs slightly over the long sides of the pan. Spritz generously with vegetable oil spray. Preheat the air fryer to 350°F.

**3.** In a large bowl, combine the beet puree, melted chocolate, syrup, egg, and vanilla. Whisk until thoroughly combined. Add the almond flour, cocoa powder, baking soda, baking powder, and salt. Stir just until combined, with no floury streaks.

**4.** Transfer the brownie batter to the prepared loaf pan and use the back of a spoon to spread it evenly in the bottom of the pan. Sprinkle with the remaining 2 tablespoons of chocolate chips and carefully place the pan in the air fryer basket.

**5.** Air fry for 18 to 20 minutes, until the brownies are firm. Transfer the pan to a wire rack to cool completely. Remove the brownies from the pan by lifting the parchment paper that hangs over the sides. Let cool and then cut into six slices. Cut each slice in half for squares.

*Per serving (2 brownies): 110 calories, 4 g protein, 13 g carbohydrates, 7 g fat (2.4 g sat fat), 3 g fiber*

# fancy, fruity & fun flavors

# Blueberry-Ricotta Phyllo Cups

**Makes 12 cups** • **Prep time: 10 minutes** • **Total time: 15 minutes**

12 frozen phyllo cups

1 tablespoon unsalted butter, melted

1 cup part-skim ricotta, drained

2 tablespoons honey

1 cup fresh blueberries

Powdered sugar, for dusting (optional)

Need a super-fast dessert idea? Keep a package of ready-made phyllo cups in your freezer to pop in the air fryer and you're just minutes away from these refreshing treats. If you're not a blueberry fan, substitute your favorite fresh fruit. Just about anything goes with ricotta. Bonus: Fruit-filled phyllo cups look gorgeous to display on a serving table.

**1.** Brush the phyllo cups with the melted butter and arrange in a single layer in the air fryer basket. Air fry at 300°F for 3 to 5 minutes, until golden brown. Transfer the cups to a serving platter and let cool to room temperature.

**2.** Meanwhile, in the work bowl of a food processor, combine the ricotta and honey. Pulse for 15 to 30 seconds, until the ricotta is whipped and smooth.

**3.** To assemble the cups, spoon a generous tablespoon of the ricotta mixture into the center of each cup. Top with fresh berries and serve dusted with powdered sugar (if using).

**Per serving (3 cups):** *210 calories, 9 g protein, 23 g carbohydrates, 9 g fat (4.9 g sat fat), 1 g fiber*

# Lemon Bars

**Makes 6 servings** • **Prep time: 10 minutes** • **Total time: 30 minutes**

## CRUST

¾ cup almond flour

2 tablespoons unsalted butter, melted

1 tablespoon pure maple syrup

Pinch of salt

## FILLING

2 large eggs

2 tablespoons unsalted butter, melted

2 tablespoons honey

¼ cup fresh lemon juice

Zest of 1 lemon

## GARNISH

1 tablespoon powdered sugar

There's so much to love about these lemon bars! Maple syrup and honey balance out the natural tartness of the lemon while still letting those sour notes take center stage. And when you make a batch in the air fryer, you'll have just the right amount to satisfy your cravings.

**1.** Line a 9 x 5-inch loaf pan with a piece of parchment so that the paper hangs slightly over the long sides of the pan. Spritz generously with vegetable oil spray. Preheat the air fryer to 350°F.

**2.** To make the crust: In a medium bowl, whisk together the almond flour, butter, maple syrup, and salt until a soft dough forms. Press the dough into the bottom of the prepared pan, about ¼ inch thick. Carefully place the pain in the air fryer basket and air fry for 15 minutes, or until just golden brown around the edges. Remove from the air fryer and allow the crust to cool while you make the filling.

**3.** To make the filling: In the bowl of a stand mixer fitted with a whisk attachment, whip the eggs for 2 to 3 minutes, until pale. Slowly add the butter and honey and mix until combined. Use a silicone spatula to fold in the lemon juice and zest until thoroughly combined.

**4.** Pour the filling into the cooled crust and bake for another 20 to 25 minutes, or until set at the edges and just barely jiggly in the center. Let the bars cool and set completely in the pan, then use the parchment paper overhanging the sides of the pan to lift them out. Dust with powdered sugar and cut into 6 servings.

*Per serving: 210 calories, 6 g protein, 15 g carbohydrates, 14 g fat (5.4 g sat fat), 1 g fiber*

# Strawberry Chimichangas

**Makes 6 servings** • **Prep time: 15 minutes** • **Total time: 20 minutes**

1 (8-ounce) package Neufchâtel cheese, softened

¼ cup nonfat Greek yogurt

½ cup sugar, divided

1 teaspoon lemon zest

1 teaspoon pure vanilla extract

1½ cups diced strawberries

6 (8-inch) whole-wheat flour tortillas

1 tablespoon unsalted butter, melted

¼ teaspoon ground cinnamon

Who would ever guess that making dessert could call for whole-wheat tortillas? After you try these fruit-filled chimichangas, you will want to try the tortillas paired with all kinds of fresh diced fruits. The secret ingredients make it simple to work a little nutrition into your sweet treats, and they crisp nicely in your air fryer.

**1.** In the bowl of a stand mixer fitted with a paddle attachment, beat the Neufchâtel, yogurt, ¼ cup of the sugar, lemon zest, and vanilla until thoroughly combined. Fold in the strawberries.

**2.** To assemble the chimichangas, arrange the tortillas on a flat surface and spread about 2 generous tablespoons of the cheese filling in the center, leaving a 1-inch border.

**3.** Working one at a time, fold one edge of the tortilla over the center, followed by the sides, and then roll up tightly like a burrito, making sure that all of the filling is enclosed. Arrange the chimichangas seam-side down in the air fryer basket and brush with the melted butter.

**4.** Air fry at 400°F for 5 minutes, pausing halfway through the cooking time to turn the chimichangas, until the tortillas are lightly browned and crisp.

**5.** In a shallow bowl, combine the remaining ¼ cup of sugar and the cinnamon. Roll the chimichangas in the cinnamon-sugar mixture just before serving.

*Per serving: 330 calories, 9 g protein, 41 g carbohydrates, 15 g fat (8.1 g sat fat), 5 g fiber*

# Strawberry Shortcake

**Makes 4 servings** • **Prep time: 15 minutes** • **Total time: 30 minutes**

¾ cup all-purpose flour, plus more for dusting

2 tablespoons sugar

1 tablespoon lemon zest

¾ teaspoon baking powder

¼ teaspoon salt + a pinch, divided

2 tablespoons cold butter

¼ cup buttermilk

2 cups sliced strawberries

1 tablespoon honey

Nondairy whipped topping (optional)

Nothing says summer like strawberry shortcake! But who wants to heat up an oven in the height of the season to bake the shortcakes? Your air fryer is the perfect solution for creating a delicious base for those berries.

**1.** Preheat the air fryer to 400°F.

**2.** In a large bowl, combine and whisk the flour, sugar, lemon zest, baking powder, and ¼ teaspoon of the salt.

**3.** Using a pastry cutter, fork, or two knives, blend the butter into the flour mixture until it resembles pea-size crumbs.

**4.** Add the buttermilk to the flour mixture. Stir just until a crumbly dough forms, taking care not to overmix.

**5.** Turn the dough out onto a lightly floured work surface and knead it gently until a shaggy dough forms. Shape the dough into a disk ½ inch thick. Cut the dough into four equal-size wedges.

**6.** Carefully arrange the shortcakes in the air fryer basket so they are not touching. Air fry for 12 to 15 minutes, until golden brown. Transfer to a wire rack to cool.

**7.** While the shortcakes are in the air fryer, prepare the strawberries. In a large bowl, combine the strawberries, honey, and remaining pinch of salt, tossing until the berries are thoroughly coated.

**8.** To serve, split the shortcakes and place the bottom halves on dessert plates. Top with the strawberries, shortcake tops, and whipped topping (if using).

*Per serving: 210 calories, 4 g protein, 36 g carbohydrates, 7 g fat (3.9 g sat fat), 2 g fiber*

# Roasted Mango Trifle

**Makes 6 servings • Prep time: 15 minutes • Total time: 25 minutes**

3 large mangoes, peeled, pitted, and cut into 1-inch chunks (about 3 cups)

1 tablespoon lime juice

2 tablespoons packed brown sugar

½ premade angel food cake, cut into 2-inch pieces

1 (8-ounce) container frozen light nondairy whipped topping, thawed

Ready to try some mango magic? Just a few minutes and your air fryer are all you need to transform a juicy mango into an intense (and naturally sweet) filling for this easy-to-assemble trifle. For a rustic presentation, create individual portions and serve them in mason jars.

**1.** In a baking dish that fits your air fryer, toss the mango with the lemon juice and brown sugar until thoroughly coated.

**2.** Place the dish in the air fryer basket and air fry at 380°F for 8 to 10 minutes, pausing halfway through the cooking time to stir the mango, until golden brown and slightly caramelized around the edges. Let cool to room temperature.

**3.** To assemble the trifle: In an 8-cup glass serving dish (or four 16-ounce mason jars), place a third of the angel food cake in the bottom of the dish. Top with half of the mangoes and any accumulated juices, followed by a third of the whipped topping. Repeat with the remaining ingredients and use the back of a spoon to smooth the top layer of whipped topping.

*Per serving: 275 calories, 4 g protein, 55 g carbohydrates, 6 g fat (4.5 g sat fat), 3 g fiber*

# Ginger-Peach Crisp

**Makes 4 servings · Prep time: 15 minutes · Total time: 30 minutes**

2 cups frozen chopped peaches, thawed

3 tablespoons all-purpose flour, divided

2 tablespoons granulated sugar

1 teaspoon lemon juice

1 tablespoon freshly grated ginger

1 teaspoon pure vanilla extract

½ cup quick oats

3 tablespoons butter, melted

3 tablespoons packed light brown sugar

Crisps are an amazing way to dress up fruit for dessert, and your air fryer does an especially efficient job of creating delicious results without overheating your kitchen. If you have access to fresh peaches, use them. But because summer peaches have a short growing season, rest assured that frozen peaches will offer the same nutritional benefits and flavor for year-round enjoyment.

**1.** In a 6-cup baking dish, combine the peaches, 1 tablespoon of the flour, granulated sugar, lemon juice, ginger, and vanilla.

**2.** In a bowl, combine the oats, butter, brown sugar, and remaining 2 tablespoons of flour. Stir with a fork until the mixture resembles coarse crumbs. Sprinkle evenly over the fruit mixture.

**3.** Place the baking dish in the air fryer basket and air fry at 350°F for 15 minutes, until golden brown and bubbling around the edges.

**4.** Let the crisp cool on a wire rack. Serve warm.

*Per serving: 305 calories, 3 g protein, 54 g carbohydrates, 10 g fat (5.6 g sat fat), 3 g fiber*

# Blue Cheese Baked Pears

**Makes 4 servings** · **Prep time: 5 minutes** · **Total time: 20 minutes**

2 large pears, halved

2 tablespoons packed brown sugar

¼ cup crumbled blue cheese (about 2 ounces)

2 tablespoons chopped walnuts

1 tablespoon balsamic glaze (optional)

If you enjoy sweet and savory flavor combinations, fruit and cheese is a classic pairing. Your air fryer helps render fresh pears into the perfect melt-in-your mouth consistency. And given the strong flavor of blue cheese, you don't need a lot to get a big impact. If you prefer, a small slice of Brie would work just as well.

**1.** Use a melon baller to scoop the seeds out of each pear half; pack about 1½ teaspoons of brown sugar into each cavity that you've created.

**2.** Place the pear halves in the air fryer basket and air fry at 380°F for 8 to 10 minutes, until golden brown and slightly brown around the edges.

**3.** Open the air fryer and sprinkle the pear halves with the blue cheese and walnuts. Air fry for another minute or two, until the cheese is melted.

**4.** Place the pears on a serving plate and let cool to room temperature. Serve drizzled with the balsamic glaze (if using).

*Per serving: 170 calories, 4 g protein, 25 g carbohydrates, 7 g fat (2.9 g sat fat), 4 g fiber*

# Blueberry Cobbler

**Makes 4 servings  •  Prep time: 15 minutes  •  Total time: 45 minutes**

2 cups blueberries

½ teaspoon fresh
lemon juice

1½ teaspoons
cornstarch

½ cup all-purpose flour

3 tablespoons sugar

½ teaspoon
baking powder

¼ teaspoon
ground nutmeg

1 tablespoon
vegetable oil

1 large egg

If you prefer a cobbler with a biscuit-like topping, this recipe is for you. With lots of natural berry sweetness and just a touch of sugar, it won't break any calorie budget. Not a blueberry fan? Feel free to substitute another juicy berry or stone fruit instead. Whatever you choose, your air fryer is guaranteed to deliver great results.

**1.** Lightly coat a 6-cup baking dish that fits in your air fryer with a spritz of vegetable oil.

**2.** Combine the blueberries, lemon juice, and cornstarch in the prepared baking dish, tossing gently until the berries are evenly coated.

**3.** In a bowl, combine the flour, sugar, baking powder, and nutmeg. Whisk until thoroughly combined. Add the vegetable oil and egg and stir just until the dough is combined.

**4.** Dollop the dough over the berries, covering as evenly as possible. Place the dish in the air fryer basket and air fry at 350°F for 30 to 40 minutes, until the dough is golden brown and the cobbler is bubbling around the edges. Remove to a wire rack to cool slightly before serving warm.

*Per serving: 185 calories, 4 g protein, 32 g carbohydrates, 5 g fat (0.7 g sat fat), 2 g fiber*

# Cherry Clafouti

**Makes 2 servings** • **Prep time: 10 minutes** • **Total time: 40 minutes**

1 cup pitted
Bing cherries

1 large egg

¼ cup reduced-
fat milk

2 tablespoons
granulated sugar

1 teaspoon pure
vanilla extract

¼ teaspoon pure
almond extract

3 tablespoons flour

1 tablespoon powdered
sugar (optional)

If you're not familiar with clafouti (sometimes called clafoutis), it's time to get to know this rustic French dessert and introduce it to your air fryer. The texture is somewhere between flan and a puffed pancake, and the result, with a mildly sweet taste, is extraordinary. If fresh cherries are not in season, frozen will work nicely, too—just make sure to pat them dry so your air fryer can deliver the best results.

**1.** Preheat the air fryer to 320°F. Lightly spritz a 6-inch cake pan with vegetable oil and add the cherries.

**2.** In a small bowl, whisk together the egg, milk, granulated sugar, vanilla, and almond extract until smooth. Slowly whisk in the flour and pour the mixture over the cherries.

**3.** Carefully place the pan in the air fryer basket and air fry for 30 minutes, or until the edges are golden brown and slightly puffed. Allow to cool for 10 minutes before slicing. Dust with powdered sugar (if using) and serve warm.

*Per serving: 190 calories, 6 g protein, 36 g carbohydrates, 3 g fat (1.2 g sat fat), 2 g fiber*

# Raspberry Betty

**Makes 4 servings** • **Prep time: 10 minutes** • **Total time: 25 minutes**

¼ cup sugar

¼ cup apricot jam, softened in the microwave for about 20 seconds

3 tablespoons butter, melted

12 ounces fresh or frozen raspberries

1 cup crumbled vanilla wafers

Similar to a cobbler or crisp, this fruity comfort-food treat will never go out of style! The appeal goes beyond taste—with just five ingredients, it's simple to put together anytime. And it makes sweet use of fiber-filled raspberries, whether abundant and fresh in season or conveniently frozen. It's worth fitting this dessert into a balanced day's menu.

**1.** Preheat the air fryer to 320°F. Spritz four 8- to 10-ounce ramekins with vegetable spray and set aside.

**2.** In a medium bowl, combine the sugar, jam, and butter. Stir until smooth. Add the raspberries and crumbled cookies, folding until the cookies are coated with the jam mixture.

**3.** Divide the mixture among the prepared ramekins and carefully place in the air fryer basket. Air fry for 15 to 20 minutes, until the tops are golden brown and small bubbles appear around the edges. Remove to a wire rack to cool slightly before serving warm.

*Per serving: 320 calories, 2 g protein, 52 g carbohydrates, 13 g fat (6.8 g sat fat), 6 g fiber*

# Oatmeal-Persimmon Pudding

**Makes 4 servings** • **Prep time: 10 minutes** • **Total time: 30 minutes**

¾ cup persimmon pulp (from about 3 very ripe Fuyu persimmons)

2 large eggs

½ cup reduced-fat cottage cheese

1 teaspoon orange zest

½ cup old-fashioned oats

4 teaspoons packed brown sugar

Dash of ground cinnamon

Persimmons are relatively low in calories and high in fiber, so pairing them with oatmeal makes this dessert an exceptionally good choice if healthier desserts are your goal. Persimmon pulp is often sold frozen, but to make your own simply cut the tops off the fruit, scoop out the flesh, and pulse in a food processor for about 30 seconds, until smooth.

**1.** Preheat the air fryer to 320°F. Spritz four 8-ounce ramekins with vegetable oil.

**2.** In a bowl, combine the persimmon pulp, eggs, cottage cheese, and orange zest, stirring until thoroughly combined. Stir in the oats.

**3.** Divide the mixture among the prepared ramekins. Top with the brown sugar and cinnamon.

**4.** Arrange the ramekins in the air fryer basket and air fry for 20 to 25 minutes, until the tops are brown. Remove to a wire rack and let cool for 5 minutes before loosening the edges with a knife and turning out onto a plate. Serve warm.

*Per serving: 200 calories, 9 g protein, 36 g carbohydrates, 4 g fat (1.1 g sat fat), 6 g fiber*

# Air-Fried Pineapple Slices

**Makes 2 servings** • **Prep time: 5 minutes** • **Total time: 20 minutes**

2 tablespoons
brown sugar

⅛ teaspoon
ground allspice

4 thick slices fresh
pineapple

2 tablespoons
crème fraîche

Fresh mint leaves,
for garnish

Just a small amount of brown sugar helps your air fryer render these pineapple slices tender and caramelized. Crème fraîche is a higher-fat version of sour cream that pairs beautifully with the intense sweetness of the fruit. However, if you prefer to keep things light, reduced-fat sour cream or Greek yogurt will work, too.

**1.** Preheat the air fryer to 380°F.

**2.** In a small bowl, mix the brown sugar and allspice with a fork.

**3.** Sprinkle half the sugar mixture over one side of the pineapple rings.

**4.** Carefully arrange the pineapple in the air fryer basket, sugar-side up, and air fry for about 8 minutes. Flip the rings, top with the remaining sugar mixture, and continue to air fry for 8 more minutes, until the pineapple is golden brown.

**5.** Serve warm topped with crème fraîche and fresh mint.

*Per serving: 270 calories, 2 g protein, 57 g carbohydrates, 6 g fat (3.5 g sat fat), 5 g fiber*

# Cinnamon-Sugar Peaches

**Makes 2 servings** • **Prep time: 5 minutes** • **Total time: 15 minutes**

2 large peaches

1 teaspoon olive oil

1 tablespoon unsalted butter, softened

2 tablespoons packed brown sugar

¼ teaspoon ground cinnamon

Pinch of salt

⅔ cup reduced-fat vanilla ice cream (optional)

2 tablespoons chopped hazelnuts (optional)

You can release the sweet flavor of traditionally grilled peaches without prepping a charcoal grill or standing over a hot gas grill. Turn to your air fryer! Just be sure to use fresh peaches. If you buy some that are still a bit underripe, enclose them in a paper bag and let them sit on the counter for a day or two to speed the ripening process.

**1.** Preheat the air fryer to 350°F.

**2.** Cut the peaches in half and remove the pits. Brush the cut sides of the peaches with oil and place skin-side down in the air fryer basket. Air fry for 5 minutes.

**3.** Meanwhile, in a small bowl, combine the butter, brown sugar, cinnamon, and salt. Mash with a fork until thoroughly combined.

**4.** Open the air fryer basket and spoon a quarter of the butter mixture into the pit cavity of each peach halve. Continue to air fry for another 5 minutes, until the peaches are caramelized on top.

**5.** Serve warm topped with ice cream and hazelnuts (if using).

*Per serving: 175 calories, 2 g protein, 26 g carbohydrates, 8 g fat (4 g sat fat), 3 g fiber*

# cookie cravings

# Small-Batch Chocolate Chip Cookies

**Makes 1 dozen cookies** • **Prep time: 10 minutes** • **Total time: 25 minutes**

2 tablespoons unsalted butter, softened

2 tablespoons packed brown sugar

2 tablespoons granulated sugar

½ teaspoon pure vanilla extract

1 egg

1¼ cups almond flour

⅛ teaspoon baking soda

Pinch of salt

½ cup semisweet chocolate chips

It's tough to withstand the temptation of a large batch of freshly baked cookies hanging around. So why not bake a smaller batch and tuck away any extras? Your air fryer makes it incredibly easy to enjoy just a few cookies at a time. Stash the remaining unbaked cookies in your freezer so they're ready to pop in the air fryer whenever you want.

**1.** In a large bowl, combine the butter, sugars, and vanilla and beat until smooth. Add the egg and continue beating until smooth. Mix in the almond flour, baking soda, and salt and stir until a stiff dough forms. Stir in the chocolate chips.

**2.** Divide the dough into twelve balls and flatten slightly into disks. Working in batches if necessary, arrange the desired number of cookies on top of a piece of parchment paper (allow about 1 inch of space between the cookies) and place in the air fryer basket.

**3.** Air fry at 350°F for 12 minutes or until the cookies are golden brown. Transfer to a cooling rack and let cool completely before serving.

**4.** To freeze unbaked cookies, place the dough disks on a plate in the freezer. When hard, transfer to a resealable freezer bag and store in the freezer for up to a month. To bake the frozen cookies, add 3 minutes to the baking time.

*Per cookie: 140 calories, 4 g protein, 13 g carbohydrates, 9 g fat (2.6 g sat fat), 1 g fiber*

# Gluten-Free Chocolate-Chip Skillet Cookie

**Makes 4 servings** • **Prep time: 10 minutes** • **Total time: 30 minutes**

4 tablespoons unsalted butter

1 cup chickpea flour

¼ cup sugar

¼ teaspoon baking soda

¼ teaspoon salt

1 large egg

1 teaspoon pure vanilla extract

¼ cup semisweet chocolate chips

While not as light in calories as other cookies, this treat gives you 3 grams of fiber and 7 grams of protein that make it worth a splurge. Plus, it's fun to share with friends! If a cast-iron skillet won't fit into your air fryer, divide the dough into four pieces, roll into balls, and then flatten slightly onto a piece of parchment paper to slip into the air fryer basket. Your cookies will bake in about half the time, but watch carefully, as times can vary.

**1.** Preheat the air fryer to 350°F.

**2.** In a 6-inch cast-iron skillet (if using) or a small pan, melt the butter over medium-low heat. Set aside.

**3.** In a large bowl, combine the chickpea flour, sugar, baking soda, and salt. Stir until thoroughly combined.

**4.** In a separate bowl, combine the egg, melted butter, and vanilla. Whisk with a fork until thoroughly combined.

**5.** Pour the egg mixture into the flour mixture and stir until thoroughly combined. Add the chocolate chips and stir until they are evenly mixed in the dough.

**6.** Transfer the dough to the cast-iron skillet. Use the back of a spoon to evenly press the dough into the skillet.

**7.** Place the skillet in the air fryer basket and air fry about 20 minutes, or until the cookie is golden brown and cooked all the way through. Let cool slightly before serving warm.

*Per serving: 310 calories, 7 g protein, 33 g carbohydrates, 17 g fat (9.7 g sat fat), 3 g fiber*

# Cranberry-Polenta Cookies

**Makes 3 dozen cookies** • **Prep time: 15 minutes** • **Total time: 25 minutes + refrigeration time**

1 cup all-purpose flour, plus more for dusting

½ cup yellow cornmeal

½ teaspoon baking powder

⅛ teaspoon salt

6 tablespoons unsalted butter, softened

⅓ cup sugar

½ teaspoon pure vanilla or almond extract

1 large egg

1 tablespoon orange zest

¼ cup dried cranberries, finely chopped

With just 50 calories and 2 grams of fat, these Italian-style cookies rise to the occasion when you want to serve a sweet but light treat after dinner. Even better, the cookie dough can be safely tucked away in the fridge for up to a week, so you can bake them fresh as desired. Your air fryer is always ready for your next dessert adventure.

**1.** In a bowl, whisk together the flour, cornmeal, baking powder, and salt. Set aside.

**2.** In the bowl of a stand mixer fitted with a paddle attachment, beat the butter and sugar until light and fluffy. Beat in the vanilla, egg, and orange zest. With the mixer on low, gradually add the flour mixture; beat until just combined. Stir in the cranberries.

**3.** Transfer the dough to a lightly floured surface; shape it into a 9-inch-long log. Wrap the dough in parchment; form it into a rectangle by flattening the top and sides with your hands. Twist the ends of the parchment paper to seal. Refrigerate until firm, at least 1 hour.

**4.** Cut a piece of parchment paper to fit the air fryer basket and set aside. Preheat the air fryer to 350°F.

**5.** Slice the dough into thirty-six ¼-inch-thick pieces and arrange on the parchment paper. (Work in batches as necessary, depending on the size of your air fryer.) Carefully place the parchment paper in the air fryer basket. Air fry for 10 to 12 minutes, until the cookies are firm to the touch. Transfer the cookies to a wire rack to cool completely.

*Per cookie: 50 calories, 1 g protein, 6 g carbohydrates, 2 g fat (1.3 g sat fat), 0 g fiber*

# Mexican Wedding Cookies

**Makes 1 dozen cookies • Prep time: 25 minutes • Total time: 45 minutes + refrigeration time**

½ cup pecans

½ cup unsalted butter, softened

1 cup powdered sugar, divided

½ teaspoon pure vanilla extract

1 cup all-purpose flour

¼ teaspoon kosher salt

Skinny air frying and eating are very much about balance, with room for splurges now and then. (Constant denial can backfire!) These are definitely cookies designed for special occasions, but if you can stick to having just one or two they're hardly likely to derail your calorie or fat budget. Using real ingredients like butter and powdered sugar ensures you'll enjoy every bite.

**1.** Place the nuts in a single layer in the air fryer basket. Air fry at 400°F for 2 minutes, pausing halfway through the cooking time to shake the basket, until the nuts are fragrant. Tip the nuts onto a plate and let cool.

**2.** Transfer the nuts to a quart-size resealable plastic bag. Seal the bag, and then use a rolling pin to roll and crush the nuts into a chunky powder. Set aside until needed.

**3.** In the bowl of stand mixer fitted with a paddle attachment, beat the butter, ⅓ cup of the powdered sugar, and vanilla on medium speed until fluffy.

**4.** Reduce the mixer speed to low and slowly add the flour and salt until the flour is thoroughly incorporated into the butter mixture. Add the crushed nuts and mix again until thoroughly incorporated.

**5.** Scrape the dough onto a piece of plastic wrap and flatten into a disk about 1 inch thick. Wrap tightly in plastic wrap and place in the refrigerator for at least 1 hour, or until the dough is firm.

**6.** Place the remaining ⅔ cup of powdered sugar in a shallow bowl. Set aside.

**7.** Remove the chilled dough from the refrigerator and form into twelve 1-inch balls. (If necessary, let the dough soften at room temperature for a few minutes.)

**8.** Roll the dough balls in the powdered sugar and arrange in the air fryer basket, spaced slightly apart. (Do not discard the remaining powdered sugar.) Air fry at 350°F for 17 to 19 minutes, or until the cookies start to brown slightly on top and are golden brown on the bottom. Let the cookies cool in the air fryer basket for 5 minutes.

**9.** While the cookies are still warm, roll them in the remaining powdered sugar. Transfer the cookies to a wire rack to cool completely.

*Per cookie: 165 calories, 2 g protein, 16 g carbohydrates, 11 g fat (5.1 g sat fat), 1 g fiber*

# Tahini Shortbread Cookies

**Makes 3 dozen cookies** • **Prep time: 15 minutes** • **Total time: 25 minutes + refrigeration time**

½ cup salted butter, softened

½ cup tahini

½ cup powdered sugar

½ teaspoon pure vanilla extract

1¾ cups all-purpose flour

½ cup toasted sesame seeds (optional)

Tahini is a smooth paste, similar to peanut butter, that is made from sesame seeds and used extensively in Middle Eastern cooking. In these cookies, the tahini works to complement the butter and provide a unique twist on traditional shortbread.

**1.** In the bowl of a stand mixer fitted with a paddle attachment, beat the butter, tahini, and powdered sugar until fluffy. Add the vanilla and beat until thoroughly combined.

**2.** Using a wooden spoon or silicone spatula to mix the dough, add the flour, a little at a time, until well combined. Transfer the dough to a piece of parchment paper and use your hands to shape it into a 9-inch-long log. Sprinkle with the sesame seeds (if using) until well coated.

**3.** Wrap the log in parchment paper, twisting at each end, and chill in the refrigerator for at least 1 hour or overnight.

**4.** Preheat the air fryer to 350°F. Cut a fresh piece of parchment paper to fit the bottom of the air fryer basket.

**5.** Slice the log into thirty-six ¼-inch-thick pieces and place on the parchment paper about 2 inches apart. (Work in batches as necessary, depending on the size of your air fryer.) Carefully place the parchment in the air fryer basket and air fry for 8 to 10 minutes, or until the cookies are firm and lightly golden.

**6.** Let the cookies cool in the basket for about 10 minutes. Transfer the cookies to a wire rack to cool completely.

*Per cookie: 70 calories, 1 g protein, 7 g carbohydrates, 4 g fat (1.9 g sat fat), 0 g fiber*

# Gluten-Free Almond Cookies

**Makes 1½ dozen cookies** • **Prep time: 10 minutes** • **Total time: 35 minutes**

2 cups almonds,
preferably unsalted

1 cup sugar

2 egg whites

½ teaspoon
almond extract

No almond flour in your pantry? No problem! This recipe relies on your food processor to transform a few cups of nuts and some other basic ingredients you are sure to have around into the easiest cookie dough ever. Next to your air fryer, a good food processor is an especially useful appliance to have on hand.

**1.** Cut a piece of parchment paper to fit the bottom of the air fryer basket and set aside. Preheat the air fryer to 300°F.

**2.** In a food processor, whirl the almonds into a fine meal. Add the sugar and whirl for another 15 seconds. Finally, add the egg whites and almond extract, then whirl for another 15 seconds, until a smooth dough forms around the blade.

**3.** Using a teaspoon, shape the dough into eighteen equal portions. Arrange the cookies on the parchment paper about 1 inch apart. (Work in batches as necessary, depending on the size of your air fryer.) Carefully place the parchment in the air fryer basket. Air fry for 25 to 30 minutes, pausing halfway through the baking time to flatten the cookies slightly with the back of a spoon, until golden.

**4.** Transfer the cookies to a wire rack to cool completely.

*Per cookie: 135 calories, 4 g protein, 15 g carbohydrates, 8 g fat (0.6 g sat fat), 2 g fiber*

# Walnut Thumbprint Cookies

**Makes 1 dozen cookies** • **Prep time: 15 minutes** • **Total time: 35 minutes**

½ cup unsalted butter, softened

⅓ cup sugar

1 teaspoon pure vanilla extract

1 cup all-purpose flour

⅛ teaspoon salt

1 large egg white, lightly beaten

½ cup walnuts, chopped

¼ cup fruit preserves (any flavor)

You can use any fruit preserve you prefer in this recipe, but sticking to something sweetened with fruit juice concentrate is a good way to avoid high fructose corn syrup. And there's no need to toast the walnuts beforehand—your air fryer will do a marvelous job for you.

**1.** Cut a piece of parchment paper to fit the air fryer basket and set aside. Preheat the air fryer to 350°F.

**2.** In the bowl of a stand mixer fitted with a paddle attachment, beat the butter, sugar, and vanilla on medium-high speed until fluffy, 2 to 3 minutes. Add the flour and salt and beat until just combined.

**3.** Divide the dough into twelve equal balls. Dip each ball in the egg white, then roll in the chopped walnuts. Press the nuts to adhere to the dough. Place on the parchment paper about 2 inches apart. (Work in batches as necessary, depending on the size of your air fryer.)

**4.** Carefully place the parchment paper in the air fryer basket. Air fry for about 12 minutes, until the cookies are puffy.

**5.** Move the air fryer basket to a heatproof surface. Use the blunt round end of a wooden spoon to make an indentation in the cookie centers. Carefully spoon about 1 teaspoon of preserves into each indentation. Continue to air fry for 2 to 3 minutes, or until the edges are golden brown.

**6.** Let the cookies cool in the air fryer basket for 5 minutes before transferring them to wire racks to cool completely.

*Per cookie: 170 calories, 2 g protein, 17 g carbohydrates, 11 g fat (5.2 g sat fat), 1 g fiber*

# Maple-Almond Biscotti

**Makes 16 biscotti • Prep time: 20 minutes • Total time: 1 hour**

1 cup coarsely chopped almonds

1 cup all-purpose flour

⅓ cup firmly packed brown sugar

1¼ teaspoons baking powder

¼ teaspoon salt

1 large egg

2 tablespoons pure maple syrup

2 tablespoons unsalted butter, melted

The Italian word biscotti literally means "twice-baked" because these exquisitely dunkable treats are first baked as a loaf and then sliced into individual cookies and baked again. Sound like a lot of work? You can make these treasures without hassle in your air fryer. The little extra time they require is worth it—they will last for 1 to 2 weeks in an airtight container. So much better than packaged varieties, and you control the ingredients!

**1.** Place the almonds in a single layer in the air fryer basket and air fry at 300°F for about 4 minutes, pausing halfway through the cooking time to shake the basket, until fragrant.

**2.** Meanwhile, in a large bowl, combine the flour, brown sugar, baking powder, and salt, stirring until thoroughly combined. Add the egg, maple syrup, and butter, stirring again until the dough is smooth. Fold in the toasted almonds and divide the mixture into two equal batches. Transfer each batch to a separate piece of parchment paper.

**3.** Use your hands to mold the dough into two rectangular pieces 6 inches long and about ½ inch thick. Working in batches, air fry at 360°F for 15 minutes.

**4.** When the first rectangular cookie is done baking, remove it along with the parchment paper from the fryer basket to a heatproof surface and place the second rectangular cookie in the air fryer for 15 minutes.

**5.** When the first cookie is cool enough to handle, use a serrated knife to slice it into eight ¾-inch-wide pieces.

**6.** When the second rectangular cookie is done, remove it to cool. Then load the slices from the first loaf, cut-side up, into the air fryer basket and air fry for about 10 minutes, pausing halfway through the cooking time to flip the biscotti, until lightly browned. Repeat the slicing and air frying steps with the second rectangular cookie.

**7.** As each set of slices is done, transfer the biscotti to a wire rack to cool completely.

*Per cookie: 130 calories, 3 g protein, 14 g carbohydrates, 7 g fat (1.4 g sat fat), 1 g fiber*

# Glazed Lemon Cookies

**Makes 2 dozen cookies** • **Prep time: 20 minutes** • **Total time: 1 hour and 5 minutes + refrigeration time**

1 cup all-purpose flour, plus more for dusting

1 cup white whole-wheat flour

1 tablespoon baking powder

½ teaspoon salt

½ cup granulated sugar

4 tablespoons unsalted butter, softened

1 large egg

2 tablespoons lemon zest

1 teaspoon pure vanilla extract

½ cup whole milk

¾ cup powdered sugar

1 tablespoon fresh lemon juice

These amazingly flavorful cookies get a nutrition boost by relying on white whole-wheat flour to complement regular all-purpose flour. However, you're unlikely to notice those details because the bright taste of lemon is the real attention-getter. And by making them in your air fryer, you can avoid heating up your whole kitchen in the process!

**1.** Cut a piece of parchment paper to fit the air fryer basket and set aside.

**2.** In a large bowl, whisk together the flours, baking powder, and salt until combined. Set aside.

**3.** In the bowl of a stand mixer fitted with a paddle attachment, beat the granulated sugar and butter on medium speed until fluffy. Add the egg, lemon zest, and vanilla and beat again until thoroughly combined. With the mixer on low speed, slowly add the flour mixture, stopping to scrape down the sides as needed, until the flour is thoroughly incorporated. Add the milk and mix again until the dough is smooth. Refrigerate the dough, uncovered, for 30 minutes, and then preheat the air fryer to 380°F.

**4.** Using lightly floured hands, roll the dough into twenty-four 1-inch balls. Arrange the cookies on the parchment paper about 1 inch apart. (Work in batches as necessary, depending on the size of your air fryer.) Carefully lower the parchment into the air fryer basket and air fry for 10 to 12 minutes, until the edges are lightly golden and the tops are dry to the touch. Transfer the cookies to a wire rack to cool completely.

**5.** To make the glaze: In a small bowl, combine the powdered sugar and lemon juice and stir until smooth. Drizzle the glaze over the tops of the cookies and let set before serving.

**Per cookie:** *90 calories, 2 g protein, 16 g carbohydrates, 2 g fat (1.4 g sat fat), 1 g fiber*

# Ice Cream Sandwiches

**Makes 8 sandwiches • Prep time: 15 minutes • Total time: 2½ hours + refrigeration time**

1½ cups all-purpose flour

¾ teaspoon baking powder

¼ teaspoon salt

2 tablespoons colored sprinkles, plus additional for garnish (both optional)

½ cup unsalted butter

½ cup sugar

1 large egg yolk

1 tablespoon lemon zest

½ teaspoon pure vanilla extract

1 cup sugar-free vanilla ice cream

Bring back childhood summer memories with a sweet splurge: homemade ice cream sandwiches! By making the cookies yourself in the air fryer, you get to control exactly what goes into them and experiment with your favorite flavor combinations. In case you want to use an ice cream different from the sugar-free vanilla in this recipe analysis, two cookies are 240 calories.

**1.** In a large bowl, whisk together the flour, baking powder, salt, and sprinkles (if using) until combined. Set aside.

**2.** In the bowl of a stand mixer fitted with a paddle attachment, beat the butter and sugar on medium speed until fluffy. Add the egg yolk, lemon zest, and vanilla and beat again until thoroughly combined. With the mixer on low speed, slowly add the flour mixture, stopping to scrape down the sides as needed, just until combined, with no floury streaks.

**3.** Transfer the dough to a piece of parchment paper and then use your hands to shape it into a log about 4 inches long. Wrap the log in the parchment paper, twisting at each end, and chill in the fridge for at least 1 hour or overnight.

**4.** Preheat the air fryer to 330°F and cut a fresh piece of parchment paper to fit the bottom of the air fryer basket.

**5.** Slice the log into sixteen ¼-inch pieces and place on the parchment paper, arranging them about 1 inch apart. (Work in batches as necessary, depending on the size of your air fryer.) Carefully place the parchment in the air fryer basket and air fry for 12 to 15 minutes, or until the cookies are firm and lightly golden.

**6.** Transfer the cookies to a wire rack to cool completely.

**7.** To assemble the sandwiches, place about 2 tablespoons of ice cream between two cookies. Garnish the edges with additional sprinkles (if using) and serve immediately.

**Per sandwich:** *270 calories, 3 g protein, 34 g carbohydrates, 14 g fat (8.2 g sat fat), 1 g fiber*

# Oatmeal Raisin Cookies

**Makes 2 dozen cookies** • **Prep time: 15 minutes** • **Total time: 25 minutes**

¾ cup all-purpose flour

½ teaspoon ground cinnamon

¼ teaspoon baking powder

¼ teaspoon baking soda

⅛ teaspoon salt

½ cup unsalted butter, softened

½ cup packed brown sugar

¼ cup granulated sugar

1 egg

1 teaspoon pure vanilla extract

1½ cups old-fashioned oats

½ cup raisins

An oatmeal cookie is classic. But feel free to branch out from the usual flavor partner, raisins. Try some dried cranberries or chopped dried apricots if you're feeling adventurous. Your air fryer makes it so easy to enjoy these cookies that you can experiment each time.

**1.** Cut a piece of parchment paper to fit the air fryer basket and set aside. Preheat the air fryer to 320°F.

**2.** In a large bowl, whisk together the flour, cinnamon, baking powder, baking soda, and salt until combined. Set aside.

**3.** In the bowl of a stand mixer fitted with a paddle attachment, beat the butter and sugars on medium speed until fluffy. Add the egg and vanilla and beat again until thoroughly combined. With the mixer on low speed, slowly add the flour mixture, stopping to scrape down the sides as needed, just until combined, with no floury streaks.

**4.** Add the oatmeal and raisins, mixing again on low speed just until combined, about 30 seconds.

**5.** Divide the dough into twenty-four portions and roll into balls. Place them on the parchment paper about 1 inch apart. (Work in batches as necessary, depending on the size of your air fryer.)

**6.** Carefully place the parchment in the air fryer basket and air fry for 6 to 8 minutes, or until the cookies are firm and lightly golden.

**7.** Transfer the cookies to a wire rack to cool completely.

**Per cookie:** *110 calories, 2 g protein, 16 g carbohydrates, 5 g fat (2.6 g sat fat), 1 g fiber*

# Three-Ingredient Peanut Butter Cookies

**Makes 1 dozen cookies** • **Prep time: 10 minutes** • **Total time: 20 minutes**

1 cup peanut butter

1 cup sugar

1 large egg

Yes, you read that right! You may be shocked to learn that you can make an amazing version of peanut butter cookies with only three simple ingredients. Use your favorite type of peanut butter, smooth or creamy—either delivers healthy fats. Then let your air fryer transform the simple dough balls into dessert magic in just 5 minutes.

**1.** Cut a piece of parchment paper to fit the air fryer basket and set aside. Preheat the air fryer to 350°F.

**2.** In the bowl of a stand mixer fitted with a paddle attachment, beat the peanut butter, sugar, and egg on medium speed until thoroughly combined.

**3.** Divide the dough into twelve portions and roll into balls. Place them on the parchment paper about 2 inches apart. (Work in batches as necessary, depending on the size of your air fryer.) Use the tines of a fork to flatten each cookie twice, rotating the direction of the tines 90 degrees on the second pass to make a crosshatch pattern.

**4.** Carefully place the parchment in the air fryer basket and air fry for 5 to 7 minutes, or until the cookies are firm and lightly golden.

**5.** Transfer the cookies to a wire rack to cool completely.

*Per cookie: 200 calories, 5 g protein, 22 g carbohydrates, 11 g fat (2.3 g sat fat), 1 g fiber*

# Peanut Butter & Banana Oatmeal Cookies

**Makes 10 cookies** • **Prep time: 10 minutes** • **Total time: 25 minutes**

1 ripe banana

1 cup quick oats

¼ cup creamy peanut butter

¼ cup mini chocolate chips

No butter, no eggs, no sugar? No problem! You can make unbelievably good cookies without these traditional baking ingredients. Try this recipe that is quick to put together and super wholesome. Even with just ¼ cup of mini chips, the chocolate flavor really comes through.

**1.** In a large bowl, mash the banana until smooth (a few small lumps are OK). Add the oats, peanut butter, and chocolate chips. Stir until thoroughly combined.

**2.** Place a piece of parchment paper in the bottom of the air fryer basket. Divide the dough into ten portions and roll into balls. Place them on the parchment paper about 1 inch apart. (Work in batches as necessary, depending on the size of your air fryer.) Press down just a bit to flatten them.

**3.** Air fry at 300°F for 10 or 12 minutes, until the cookies are golden brown. Carefully lift the parchment paper out of the air fryer and transfer to a wire rack. Let cool for a few minutes before serving.

*Per cookie: 140 calories, 4 g protein, 14 g carbohydrates, 8 g fat (2.2 g sat fat), 2 g fiber*

# Espresso Crinkles

**Makes 2 dozen cookies** • **Prep time: 15 minutes** • **Total time: 25 minutes + refrigeration time**

1 cup all-purpose flour

1¾ cups powdered sugar, divided

¼ cup Dutch-processed cocoa powder

1¼ teaspoons baking powder

¼ teaspoon salt

2 tablespoons canola oil

1½ ounces baking chocolate, chopped

1 teaspoon instant espresso

¾ cup packed brown sugar

3 tablespoons honey

1½ teaspoons pure vanilla extract

2 large egg whites

This is a great recipe to start the night before because the rich chocolate flavors improve with an overnight rest in the fridge. In the morning, all you need to do is form the cookies and your air fryer will finish the job for you in record time. You'll love the ease, taste, and reasonable calories and fat!

**1.** In a large bowl, whisk together the flour, ¾ cup of the powdered sugar, cocoa powder, baking powder, and salt until thoroughly combined.

**2.** In a small saucepan over low heat, combine the oil and chocolate, stirring constantly until the chocolate melts. Add the espresso and stir until blended. Remove from the heat.

**3.** Transfer the chocolate mixture to a large bowl and let cool to room temperature, about 5 minutes. Add the brown sugar, honey, and vanilla. Add the egg whites, stirring with a whisk. Add the flour mixture to the egg mixture, stirring gently just until combined. Cover; chill for at least 2 hours or overnight.

**4.** Cut a piece of parchment to fit your air fryer and set aside. Preheat the air fryer to 350°F. Divide the dough into twenty-four portions and roll into balls. Dredge the balls in the remaining ½ cup of powdered sugar. Place the balls 2 inches apart on the parchment paper. (Work in batches as necessary, depending on the size of your air fryer.)

**5.** Carefully place the parchment paper in the air fryer basket and air fry for about 10 minutes, or until the cookie tops are cracked and almost set. Let the cookies cool in the air fryer basket for about 2 minutes before transferring them to a wire rack to cool completely before serving.

*Per cookie: 105 calories, 1 g protein, 20 g carbohydrates, 2 g fat (0.8 g sat fat), 1 g fiber*

# Dark Chocolate–Avocado Cookies

**Makes 1½ dozen cookies** • **Prep time: 10 minutes** • **Total time: 20 minutes**

1 ripe avocado, peeled and pitted

¼ cup granulated sugar

¼ cup packed brown sugar

1 large egg

1 teaspoon pure vanilla extract

½ cup Dutch-processed cocoa powder

⅓ cup all-purpose flour

½ teaspoon baking soda

2 ounces dark chocolate, coarsely chopped

If cutting down on saturated fat is part of your game plan, this recipe is for you. Avocado makes a fantastic stand-in for butter in these decadent cookies while adding a smart dose of fiber. Just a hint of the best dark chocolate you can find will give them all the indulgence you need for a very satisfying cookie.

**1.** Cut a piece of parchment paper to line the air fryer and set aside. Preheat the air fryer to 350°F.

**2.** In the work bowl of a food processor, combine the avocado, sugars, egg, and vanilla. Whirl until smooth, pausing to scrape down the sides if necessary.

**3.** In a large bowl, whisk together the cocoa powder, flour, and baking soda. Transfer the avocado mixture to the flour mixture and stir just until the ingredients are thoroughly combined. Fold in the dark chocolate.

**4.** Divide the dough into eighteen portions and roll into balls. Place them on the parchment paper about 1 inch apart. (Work in batches as necessary, depending on the size of your air fryer.)

**5.** Carefully place the parchment paper in the air fryer basket and air fry for 8 to 10 minutes, or until the cookie tops are set. Let the cookies cool in the air fryer basket for about 2 minutes before transferring them to a wire rack to cool completely before serving.

*Per cookie: 70 calories, 1 g protein, 11 g carbohydrates, 3 g fat (1.2 g sat fat), 2 g fiber*

# perfect-portion cakes & pies

# Vanilla Dream Mini Cupcakes

**Makes 1 dozen cupcakes • Prep time: 5 minutes • Total time: 20 minutes**

2 tablespoons
unsalted butter

⅓ cup all-purpose flour

3 tablespoons sugar

¼ teaspoon
baking soda

⅛ teaspoon salt

1 large egg

2 tablespoons
whole milk

2 teaspoons pure
vanilla extract

¾ cup prepared
frosting (optional)

2 or 3 drops food
coloring (optional)

Indulge your cupcake cravings without going calorie crazy! Made with real butter, a little sugar, and just the right amount of vanilla extract, the batter comes together in minutes so you can enjoy these sweet bites fresh from your air fryer in no time. They're simply perfect topped with a dollop of sugar-free nondairy topping and some fresh berries, but here we've dressed them up for a party using ready-made icing and a few drops of food coloring.

**1.** Spritz a mini cupcake pan with vegetable spray. (A silicone mini cupcake pan that fits into the basket of your air fryer is the best equipment for the job; use liners for a fancier presentation.) Preheat the air fryer to 350°F.

**2.** In a large microwave-safe glass bowl, melt the butter in the microwave, heating on high in 30-second increments until melted.

**3.** Add the flour, sugar, baking soda, salt, egg, milk, and vanilla. Whisk until smooth. Fill each of the cupcake liners with a generous tablespoon of the batter.

**4.** Carefully place the mini cupcake pan in the air fryer basket. Air fry for 8 to 10 minutes, until the cupcakes rise and are golden and a wooden toothpick inserted into the center of a cupcake slides out cleanly. Let cool for a few minutes, then remove the cupcakes, transfer to a baking rack, and let cool completely.

**5.** While the cupcakes are cooling, in a small bowl, combine the frosting and food coloring (if using). Stir until the coloring is evenly distributed; use an offset spatula to spread about a tablespoon of frosting on top of each cupcake. Alternatively, transfer the frosting to a piping bag fitted with a metal tip and decorate the cupcakes as pictured.

*Per serving (2 mini cupcakes, unfrosted):* *100 calories, 2 g protein, 12 g carbohydrates, 5 g fat (2.8 g sat fat), 0 g fiber*

# Lemon Sponge Cake

**Makes 6 servings** • **Prep time: 15 minutes** • **Total time: 40 minutes**

1 cup all-purpose flour

1½ teaspoons baking powder

Pinch of salt

6 tablespoons unsalted butter, softened

⅓ cup sugar

1 teaspoon pure vanilla extract

¼ cup unsweetened applesauce

2 large eggs

2 tablespoons fresh lemon juice

¼ cup raspberry preserves

¾ cup low-fat nondairy whipped topping

½ cup fresh raspberries, for garnish (optional)

This cake is just as much at home served at an elegant garden party as on a picnic table at a backyard barbecue. It's so versatile and delicious you can serve it just about anywhere or for any occasion. If you want even more lemony oomph, use lemon curd in place of the preserves.

**1.** Preheat the air fryer to 320°F. Spritz a 7-inch cake pan lightly with vegetable oil and line with parchment paper. Set aside.

**2.** In a bowl, combine the flour, baking powder, and salt, stirring until thoroughly combined. Set aside.

**3.** In the bowl of a stand mixer fitted with a paddle attachment, beat the butter, sugar, and vanilla until fluffy. Add the applesauce and the eggs, one at a time, and beat until thoroughly combined. Stir in the lemon juice. Add the flour mixture and mix thoroughly.

**4.** Pour the batter into the prepared cake pan and use an offset spatula to smooth the top.

**5.** Carefully place the pan in the air fryer basket and air fry for 20 to 25 minutes, until lightly brown and a wooden toothpick inserted into the center of the cake slides out cleanly. Let cool for a few minutes, then release the cake, transfer to a wire rack, and let cool completely.

**6.** Split the cake horizontally to make two layers. Spread the raspberry preserves on the cut side of the bottom layer and set the top layer over it. Serve with whipped topping and raspberries (if using).

*Per serving: 260 calories, 5 g protein, 28 g carbohydrates, 15 g fat (8.9 g sat fat), 1 g fiber*

# Salted Caramel–Apple Cakes

**Makes 2 servings** • **Prep time: 10 minutes** • **Total time: 20 minutes**

¼ cup all-purpose flour

3 tablespoons sugar

½ teaspoon apple pie spice

½ teaspoon baking powder

2 tablespoons unsweetened applesauce

2 tablespoons reduced-fat milk

1 teaspoon vegetable oil

3 tablespoons prepared caramel sauce

Pinch of kosher salt

Topping desserts with a bit of salt is an age-old tip for amplifying sweetness—you only need a pinch of salt and a small drizzle of caramel sauce to taste how this trick works. Most air fryers can easily hold two ramekins, but this recipe can be doubled if you want to make a larger quantity to share.

**1.** Preheat the air fryer to 350°F. Spritz two 8- to 10-ounce ramekins lightly with vegetable oil and set aside.

**2.** In a large bowl, combine the flour, sugar, pie spice, and baking powder, stirring until thoroughly combined. Add the applesauce, milk, and oil, stirring again until the batter is smooth.

**3.** Divide the batter between the prepared ramekins and carefully place them in the air fryer basket. Air fry for 8 to 12 minutes, pausing halfway through to check their doneness, until the tops are golden brown and a wooden toothpick inserted into the center of one of the cakes slides out cleanly. Let cool for a few minutes.

**4.** To serve, drizzle with the caramel sauce and top with a pinch of salt.

*Per serving: 250 calories, 2 g protein, 53 g carbohydrates, 3 g fat (0.5 g sat fat), 1 g fiber*

# Carrot Cupcakes with Cream Cheese Frosting

**Makes 6 cupcakes** • **Prep time: 15 minutes** • **Total time: 45 minutes**

## CUPCAKES

¾ cup peeled and grated carrots, divided

½ cup all-purpose flour

½ cup granulated sugar

½ teaspoon baking soda

½ teaspoon ground cinnamon, plus more for garnish

¼ cup vegetable oil or canola oil

2 tablespoons orange juice

½ teaspoon pure vanilla extract

1 large egg

2 tablespoons shredded coconut

## FROSTING

½ (8-ounce) package Neufchâtel cheese, softened

2 tablespoons unsalted butter, softened

Pinch of salt

½ cup powdered sugar

All the delicious flavor in these satisfying cupcakes shines through in just 20 minutes from your air fryer. For a special treat, top them with the easy-to-make cream cheese frosting that is not too sweet. If you prefer to skip the frosting, you'll save about 100 calories per serving. Have fun with a taste test to try them both frosted and unfrosted!

**1.** Preheat the air fryer to 350°F. Spritz six silicone muffin cups lightly with vegetable oil and set aside. (Use liners for a fancier presentation.)

**2.** To make the cupcakes: Measure 2 tablespoons of carrots to use as garnish and set aside. In a large bowl, combine the flour, granulated sugar, baking soda, and cinnamon, stirring until thoroughly combined. Add the oil, orange juice, vanilla, and egg, stirring again until the batter is smooth. Add the remaining carrots and coconut and stir just until thoroughly combined.

**3.** Divide the batter among the prepared muffin cups and carefully place them in the air fryer basket. Air fry for 20 minutes, until the tops are golden brown and a wooden toothpick inserted into the center of one of the cakes slides out cleanly. Let cool for a few minutes, then remove the cakes, transfer to a wire rack, and let cool completely.

**4.** To make the frosting: In the bowl of a stand mixer fitted with a paddle attachment, beat the Neufchâtel, butter, and salt on medium speed until thoroughly combined. With the mixer running, slowly add the powdered sugar a few spoonfuls at a time until the frosting becomes fluffy.

**5.** Transfer the frosting to a piping bag fitted with a metal tip and decorate the cupcakes. Top with the reserved carrot.

*Per cupcake: 335 calories, 4 g protein, 38 g carbohydrates, 19 g fat (6.4 g sat fat), 1 g fiber*

# Banana Cake for Two

**Makes 2 servings • Prep time: 10 minutes • Total time: 20 minutes**

⅓ cup all-purpose flour, plus more for dusting

3 tablespoons sugar

½ teaspoon baking powder

¼ cup mashed ripe banana

2 tablespoons plain or vanilla low-fat Greek yogurt

1 tablespoon vegetable oil

2 tablespoons chopped walnuts

If you love banana bread, this simple but flavorful cake will become a fast favorite. Thanks to your air fryer, it only takes about 10 minutes to make a cake for dessert—without the kitchen overheating. It's a great way to make use of that single banana you may have lingering on the counter. So go ahead and make any weeknight a little sweeter!

**1.** Preheat the air fryer to 350°F. Spritz two 8- to 10-ounce ramekins lightly with vegetable oil and dust with flour. Set aside.

**2.** In a bowl, combine the flour, sugar, and baking powder, stirring until thoroughly combined. Add the banana, yogurt, and oil, stirring again until the batter is smooth.

**3.** Divide the batter between the prepared ramekins and top with the walnuts. Air fry for 8 to 12 minutes, pausing halfway through to check their doneness, until the tops are golden and a wooden toothpick inserted into the center of one of the cakes slides out cleanly. Let cool for a few minutes.

**4.** Run a knife along the edges of the cakes to release them from the ramekins and transfer to a wire rack to cool completely.

*Per serving: 295 calories, 6 g protein, 42 g carbohydrates, 12 g fat (1.1 g sat fat), 2 g fiber*

# Pineapple Upside-Down Cakes

**Makes 2 servings** • **Prep time: 15 minutes** • **Total time: 30 minutes**

3 tablespoons unsalted butter, divided

¼ cup reduced-fat milk

2 tablespoons granulated sugar

1 teaspoon pure vanilla extract

⅓ cup all-purpose flour

½ teaspoons baking powder

½ teaspoon salt

¼ teaspoon ground allspice

1 tablespoon packed brown sugar

2 slices canned pineapple, patted dry

2 maraschino cherries, patted dry

Did you know that this cake was first developed for a recipe contest in the 1920s? A hundred years later, it's still a winner! Nobody could have predicted how air fryers would make the tasty treat easier than ever to prepare.

**1.** Preheat the air fryer to 320°F.

**2.** Place 1 tablespoon of butter in each of two 8- to 10-ounce ramekins and the remaining 1 tablespoon in a small microwave-safe mixing bowl. Microwave the butter for 30 seconds on high until it is melted. Swirl the butter in the ramekins to coat the sides and set aside.

**3.** To the mixing bowl with the melted butter, add the milk, granulated sugar, and vanilla and whisk until thoroughly combined. Add the flour, baking powder, salt, and allspice and whisk again until just combined, with no floury streaks. Set aside.

**4.** Sprinkle the brown sugar evenly on top of the butter in the ramekins, set the pineapple slices on top, and then place a cherry in the center of each slice.

**5.** Divide the batter between the ramekins and carefully place the ramekins in the air fryer basket. Air fry for 10 to 12 minutes, until the tops are golden and a wooden toothpick inserted into the center of a cake comes out clean. Transfer the cakes to a wire rack and let cool for 5 minutes.

**6.** Run a knife along the edges of the cakes to release them from the ramekins, place a dessert plate face-down over the ramekin, and carefully invert the cake before serving.

*Per serving: 330 calories, 3 g protein, 40 g carbohydrates, 18 g fat (11 g sat fat), 1 g fiber*

# Double-Dose Chocolate Cupcakes

**Makes 8 cupcakes • Prep time: 15 minutes • Total time: 30 minutes**

1 large egg

¼ cup plain nonfat Greek yogurt

3 tablespoons reduced-fat milk

⅓ cup vegetable oil

½ teaspoon pure vanilla extract

⅓ cup sugar

¾ cup self-rising flour

¼ cup Dutch-processed cocoa powder

Pinch of salt

¾ cup dark chocolate chips, divided

These delightful cupcakes enjoy a double dose of chocolate, both in the batter and on top, so there's no need for the extra calories that frostings and glazes bring to the table. If you feel a garnish is absolutely necessary, just a light dusting of powdered sugar should do the trick.

**1.** Preheat the air fryer to 320°F. Spritz eight silicone muffin cups lightly with vegetable oil and set aside.

**2.** In a large bowl, whisk together the egg, yogurt, milk, oil, and vanilla. Add the sugar and whisk until thoroughly combined.

**3.** Sift in the flour and cocoa powder, then add the salt and ½ cup of the chocolate chips. Stir until just combined, with no floury streaks.

**4.** Divide the batter among the prepared muffin cups. Sprinkle the remaining chocolate chips on top.

**5.** Carefully arrange the cakes in the air fryer basket. (Work in batches as necessary, depending on the size of your air fryer.) Air fry for 12 to 15 minutes, until the cakes rise and a wooden toothpick inserted into the center of a cake comes out clean.

**6.** Transfer to a wire rack and let cool for at least 15 minutes before serving.

*Per cupcake: 255 calories, 5 g protein, 29 g carbohydrates, 15 g fat (4.1 g sat fat), 2 g fiber*

# Gingerbread Cake with Maple Topping

**Makes 9 servings** • **Prep time: 10 minutes** • **Total time: 30 minutes**

2½ cups all-purpose flour

1 teaspoon baking soda

1 teaspoon salt

1 teaspoon ground ginger

1 cup molasses

1 large egg

¼ cup sugar

1 cup buttermilk

2 tablespoons unsalted butter, melted

1 cup low-fat nondairy whipped topping

1 tablespoon pure maple syrup

This warm-flavored cake works best if your air fryer can accommodate a larger baking pan. If that's not an option, you can air fry in batches; simply create cupcake-style portions using silicone muffin cups (fill them two-thirds full) and adjust the baking time accordingly. Whether you make a full cake or cupcakes, your house will smell amazing!

**1.** Preheat the air fryer to 320°F. Spritz an 8 x 8-inch baking pan lightly with vegetable oil and set aside.

**2.** In a large bowl, whisk together the flour, baking soda, salt, and ginger until thoroughly combined.

**3.** Add the molasses, egg, sugar, buttermilk, and butter. Use a silicone spatula or wooden spoon to mix just until the batter is smooth, with no floury streaks.

**4.** Pour the batter into the prepared pan.

**5.** Carefully place the pan in the air fryer basket. Air fry for 20 to 25 minutes, until the cake has risen and a wooden toothpick inserted into the center comes out clean. Transfer to a wire rack and let cool for at least 15 minutes.

**6.** Meanwhile, in a bowl, stir the whipped topping and maple syrup until thoroughly combined.

**7.** Serve the cake with about 1½ tablespoons of the topping.

*Per serving: 330 calories, 6 g protein, 64 g carbohydrates, 5 g fat (3.1 g sat fat), 1 g fiber*

# Easy Almond Cake

**Makes 6 servings** • **Prep time: 15 minutes** • **Total time: 40 minutes**

¾ cup all-purpose flour

Pinch of salt

6 tablespoons unsalted butter, softened

¾ cup sugar

1 large egg

1½ teaspoons pure almond extract

½ teaspoon pure vanilla extract

2 tablespoons sliced almonds

From the time you get your mixing bowl out, you can have this cake in the air fryer in about 15 minutes flat. Then let your amazing appliance go to work. The result: a classic nutty cake that's the perfect base to top with your favorite fresh fruit. Sometimes simple is just what you need!

**1.** Preheat the air fryer to 350°F. Generously spritz a 7-inch cake pan or a 7½-inch springform pan with vegetable oil and dust with flour. Set aside.

**2.** In a small bowl, whisk together the flour and salt.

**3.** In the bowl of a mixer fitted with a paddle attachment, beat the butter and sugar on medium speed until light and creamy. Add the egg, almond extract, and vanilla and continue beating until thoroughly combined. Add the flour mixture, using a silicone spatula to fold in and scraping the sides and bottom of the bowl periodically until there are no floury streaks.

**4.** Pour the batter into the prepared pan and scatter the almonds on top. Carefully place the pan in the air fryer basket and air fry for 25 minutes, until golden brown and a wooden toothpick inserted into the center of the cake slides out cleanly.

**5.** Transfer the cake to a wire rack and let cool for about 15 minutes, then release the cake and return it to the wire rack to cool completely.

*Per serving: 280 calories, 3 g protein, 37 g carbohydrates, 14 g fat (7.7 g sat fat), 1 g fiber*

# Strawberry Tarts

**Makes 4 servings** • **Prep time: 25 minutes** • **Total time: 45 minutes + refrigeration time**

## CRUST

½ (14.1-ounce) package refrigerated pie crust dough

2 ounces Neufchâtel cheese

1 tablespoon powdered sugar

## FILLING

2½ cups thickly sliced fresh strawberries, divided

¼ cup granulated sugar

1 tablespoon cornstarch

¾ teaspoon unflavored gelatin powder

Pinch of salt

1 teaspoon fresh lemon juice

½ cup nondairy whipped topping (optional)

Have you discovered the magic in Neufchâtel cheese? This lower-fat alternative to cream cheese works flavor and nutrition profile wonders in many desserts. In this tart recipe, a thin layer of Neufchâtel cheese is an elegant pairing with strawberries—and it keeps the crust that your air fryer produces remarkably crisp!

**1.** Preheat the air fryer to 400°F.

**2.** To make the crust: Roll the dough out on a lightly floured work surface and divide into four pieces. Working one at a time, roll each piece into a circle 6 to 7 inches in diameter.

**3.** Gently place the dough in 4-inch metal tart pans, pressing firmly around the edges and trimming any dough that hangs over the edge. Prick the dough with the tines of a fork. Place a piece of parchment paper over the dough and fill the pans with ¼ cup of dried beans, rice, or pie weights.

**4.** Carefully place the tarts in the air fryer basket. (Work in batches, as necessary, depending on the size of your air fryer.) Air fry for 10 to 12 minutes, until golden. Transfer to a wire rack to cool completely.

**5.** In a small bowl, use a fork to mash the Neufchâtel until it is soft. Add the powdered sugar and mix until thoroughly combined. Set aside.

**6.** To make the filling: In a food processor, process ½ cup of the strawberries until smooth, scraping down the sides of the bowl as needed.

**7.** In a small saucepan, whisk together the granulated sugar, cornstarch, gelatin, salt, and lemon juice. Mix in the berry puree.

**8.** Cook over medium-high heat, stirring constantly with a silicone spatula, and bring to a boil. Continue boiling for 2 minutes, scraping the bottom and sides of the pan to prevent scorching. Transfer to a large bowl and let cool to room temperature.

**9.** Add the remaining 2 cups of strawberries to the mixture and fold gently with a silicone spatula until evenly coated.

**10.** To assemble the tarts: When the tart shells are completely cool, spread a thin layer of the Neufchâtel mixture on the bottom and sides. Divide the berry mixture among the tart pans. Cover and refrigerate for at least 4 hours.

**11.** Remove the tarts from the pans just before serving. Top with whipped topping (if using).

*Per serving: 325 calories, 4 g protein, 47 g carbohydrates, 16 g fat (6.8 g sat fat), 2 g fiber*

# Apple Crostata

**Makes 6 servings** • **Prep time: 15 minutes** • **Total time: 35 minutes**

2 Granny Smith apples, cored and thinly sliced

1 tablespoon fresh lemon juice

3 tablespoons packed brown sugar

1 tablespoon all-purpose flour

½ teaspoon ground cinnamon

Pinch of salt

½ (14.1-ounce) package refrigerated pie crust dough

1 tablespoon granulated sugar

This rustic tart has all of the traditional flavors of apple pie—with much less stress involved in crimping the crust. You can safely use parchment paper in your air fryer, and in this case holding the sides of the paper like a sling makes it easy to lower the crostata into the air fryer basket. However, the paper edges will become brittle after time in the air fryer, so use a large spatula to carefully remove the crostata when it's done.

**1.** Preheat the air fryer to 360°F.

**2.** In a large bowl, combine the apples and lemon juice, tossing until the apples are thoroughly coated. Place your hand over the apples and tip the bowl over the sink to drain some of the lemon juice out of the bowl.

**3.** Add the brown sugar, flour, cinnamon, and salt, tossing again until the apples are thoroughly coated.

**4.** Unroll the dough onto a piece of parchment paper and place the apples in the center, leaving a 1-inch border around the edges. Fold one edge toward the center, repeating the fold all the way around the crust to form a 1-inch edge for the crostata. Sprinkle the edge of the crust evenly with the granulated sugar.

**5.** Holding the sides of the parchment like a sling, carefully place the crostata in the air fryer basket. Air fry for 16 to 20 minutes, or until the crust is golden brown and the apples are soft.

**6.** Use a large, flat spatula to carefully remove the crostata from the air fryer and place it on a baking sheet. Let cool for 20 minutes before slicing and serving.

*Per serving:* *205 calories, 2 g protein, 33 g carbohydrates, 8 g fat (3.3 g sat fat), 2 g fiber*

# Apricot Crostata

**Makes 6 servings** • **Prep time: 15 minutes** • **Total time: 35 minutes**

6 ripe apricots
(about 12 ounces),
pitted and halved

¼ cup sugar, divided

1 tablespoon cornstarch

¼ teaspoon
ground nutmeg

Pinch of salt

½ (14.1-ounce) package
refrigerated pie crust
dough

2 tablespoons chopped
hazelnuts

Fresh apricots are a treat to behold, but they can be an expensive ingredient to use in traditional pies. A crostata, on the other hand, requires far fewer fruits, so you can make the most of this summertime luxury. In fact, you only need a half dozen apricots to prepare this truly memorable air fryer dessert.

**1.** Preheat the air fryer to 360°F.

**2.** In a large bowl, combine the apricots, 3 tablespoons of the sugar, cornstarch, nutmeg, and salt, tossing until the apricots are thoroughly coated.

**3.** Unroll the dough onto a piece of parchment paper and place the apricots in the center, leaving a 1-inch border around the edges. Fold one edge toward the center, repeating the fold all the way around the crust to form a 1-inch edge for the crostata. Top the apricots with the hazelnuts and sprinkle the edge evenly with the remaining 1 tablespoon of sugar.

**4.** Holding the sides of the parchment like a sling, carefully place the crostata in the air fryer basket. Air fry for 16 to 20 minutes, or until the crust is golden brown and the apricots are soft.

**5.** Use a large, flat spatula to carefully remove the crostata from the air fryer and place it on a baking sheet. Let cool for 20 minutes before slicing and serving.

*Per serving: 205 calories, 2 g protein, 30 g carbohydrates, 10 g fat (3.4 g sat fat), 1 g fiber*

# Cherry-Ricotta Fruit Pies

**Makes 4 servings** • **Prep time: 20 minutes** • **Total time: 35 minutes**

½ (14.1-ounce) package refrigerated pie crust dough

¼ cup part-skim ricotta

¼ cup cherry preserves

1 large egg white, lightly beaten (optional)

Craving a cherry pie? These quick-to-assemble hand pies will make you happy. You only need to have a few ingredients on hand to get these into your air fryer quickly. In fact, this dessert is just one more reason why it pays to keep a package of refrigerated pie crust dough in the fridge or freezer at the ready.

**1.** Preheat the air fryer to 400°F. Cut a piece of parchment paper to fit the bottom of your air fryer basket.

**2.** Roll the dough out on a lightly floured work surface and use a 3-inch biscuit cutter to cut eight circles. (Gather and roll the scraps again if necessary.)

**3.** Arrange four of the circles on the parchment. (Work in batches as necessary, depending on the size of your air fryer.) Spread 1 tablespoon of the ricotta in the center of each circle, leaving a ½-inch border. Spoon 1 tablespoon of the preserves over the ricotta. Top with the remaining four circles of dough. Use a fork to gently seal the edges and cut a small decorative hole in the top layer of dough. If you prefer a shiny crust, brush the tops with egg white (if using).

**4.** Carefully place the parchment in the air fryer basket. Air fry for 13 to 15 minutes, until golden. Transfer to a wire rack and let cool before serving.

*Per serving: 275 calories, 4 g protein, 38 g carbohydrates, 13 g fat (5.8 g sat fat), 0 g fiber*

# Mini Buttermilk Pies

**Makes 6 servings** • **Prep time: 20 minutes** • **Total time: 40 minutes + refrigeration time**

2 ounces Neufchâtel cheese, softened

2 tablespoons unsalted butter, softened, + 1 tablespoon melted, divided

⅓ cup + 1½ teaspoons all-purpose flour, divided

2 tablespoons plain yellow cornmeal

1 large egg

¼ cup whole buttermilk

2 tablespoons fresh lemon juice

1½ teaspoons honey

3 tablespoons sugar

This Southern classic offers just the right amount of sweetness. Neufchâtel cheese, a lower-fat alternative to cream cheese, helps make the crust especially tender and keeps the dessert to 160 calories per serving. Bless your air fryer!

**1.** Lightly spritz six silicone muffin cups with vegetable oil and set aside.

**2.** In the bowl of a stand mixer fitted with a paddle attachment, beat the Neufchâtel and the softened butter until smooth. Scrape down the sides of the bowl with a silicone spatula. Blend in the ⅓ cup of flour and the corn-meal on low speed until a dough forms. Divide the mixture into six pieces and roll into balls. Working one at a time, press the dough balls evenly on the bottom and up the sides of the prepared muffin cups. Refrigerate for 30 minutes.

**3.** Preheat the air fryer to 350°F.

**4.** In a large mixing bowl, whisk together the egg, buttermilk, lemon juice, honey, and the 1 tablespoon of melted butter. In a separate large bowl, combine the sugar and the remaining 1½ teaspoons of flour, then whisk into the buttermilk mixture. Divide the filling among the prepared muffin cups.

**5.** Carefully arrange the muffin cups in the air fryer basket. (Work in batches as necessary, depending on the size of your air fryer.) Air fry for 20 to 25 minutes, until the crust is golden and the filling is set. Let stand for 5 minutes before transferring to a wire rack to cool completely. Cover and refrigerate if you prefer to serve the pies chilled.

*Per serving: 160 calories, 4 g protein, 17 g carbohydrates, 9 g fat (5.3 g sat fat), 0 g fiber*

# Mini Key Lime Pies

Makes 6 servings • Prep time: 10 minutes • Total time: 18 minutes + refrigeration time

1 (14-ounce) can sweetened condensed milk

½ cup light sour cream

½ cup Key lime juice

1 tablespoon lime zest

6 mini graham cracker pie crusts

¾ cup low-fat nondairy whipped topping

1 Key lime, thinly sliced (optional)

The sweet-tart flavor of Key lime pie is a refreshing way to end a summer cookout! Making individual pies in your air fryer keeps your kitchen cool, simplifies serving to guests, and helps you enjoy a lighter bite of dessert with built-in portion control. And it's easy to pull together ahead of time—in just 15 minutes. It will be waiting in your fridge.

**1.** Preheat the air fryer to 350°F.

**2.** In a large bowl, whisk together the condensed milk, sour cream, lime juice, and lime zest until smooth.

**3.** Pour the filling into the graham cracker crusts, filling to the top.

**4.** Carefully arrange the pies in the air fryer basket. (Work in batches as necessary, depending on the size of your air fryer.) Air fry for 5 to 8 minutes, until the pies are only slightly jiggly. (The pies will continue to firm up as they cool.) Transfer to a wire rack to cool. Cover and refrigerate until thoroughly chilled, at least 1 hour.

**5.** To serve, garnish each mini pie with the whipped topping and a slice of lime (if using).

*Per serving: 350 calories, 10 g protein, 67 g carbohydrates, 16 g fat (10.6 g sat fat), 0 g fiber*

# Mini Pumpkin Pies

**Makes 6 servings** • **Prep time: 20 minutes** • **Total time: 45 minutes + refrigeration time**

## CRUST

2 ounces Neufchâtel cheese, softened

2 tablespoons unsalted butter, softened

½ cup all-purpose flour

Pinch of salt

## FILLING

1 cup canned pumpkin puree

½ cup sweetened condensed milk

1 large egg

½ teaspoon ground cinnamon

¼ teaspoon ground nutmeg

⅛ teaspoon ground clove

## GARNISH

½ cup low-fat nondairy whipped topping

6 seasonal sugar cookies (optional)

Thanksgiving wouldn't be complete without pumpkin pie. Serve the holiday dessert favorite in these perfect little packages. You'll celebrate the taste without any regrets about overdoing it later. Your air fryer can be an especially valuable appliance around the holidays, when your oven is filled with other seasonal dishes.

**1.** Lightly spritz six silicone muffin cups with vegetable oil and set aside.

**2.** To make the crust: In the bowl of a stand mixer fitted with a paddle attachment, beat the Neufchâtel and the softened butter until smooth. Scrape down the sides of the bowl with a silicone spatula. Blend in the flour and salt on low speed until a dough forms.

**3.** Divide the dough into six pieces and roll into balls. Working one at a time, press the dough balls evenly on the bottom and all the way up the sides of the prepared muffin cups. Refrigerate for 30 minutes.

**4.** Preheat the air fryer to 300°F.

**5.** To make the filling: In a large bowl, combine the pumpkin puree, condensed milk, egg, cinnamon, nutmeg, and clove. Stir until smooth. Divide the filling among the muffin cups, leaving a small edge of crust at the top (you may have a little left over).

**6.** Carefully arrange the muffin cups in the air fryer basket. (Work in batches as necessary, depending on the size of your air fryer.) Air fry for 12 to 15 minutes, until the crust is golden and the filling is set. Let the pies rest in the air fryer for 10 minutes before transferring them to a wire rack to cool completely.

**7.** Top with whipped topping and garnish with seasonal cookies (if using).

*Per serving:* 235 calories, 6 g protein, 34 g carbohydrates, 9 g fat
(5.3 g sat fat), 4 g fiber

# index